D0600682

ESCAPE TO THE

American Desert

Photography by Catherine Karnow
Text by David Lansing

Fodor's

FODOR'S TRAVEL PUBLICATIONS
NEW YORK • TORONTO • LONDON • SYDNEY • AUCKLAND • WWW.FODORS.COM

Escape to the American Desert
COPYRIGHT © 2002 BY FODORS LLC
Photographs copyright © 2001 by Catherine Karnow
Fodor's is a registered trademark of Random House, Inc.

All rights reserved under International and Pan-American Copyright Conventions. Published in the United States by Fodor's Travel Publications, a unit of Fodors LLC, a subsidiary of Random House, Inc., and simultaneously in Canada by Random House of Canada Limited, Toronto. Distributed by Random House, Inc., New York.

No illustrations or other portions of this book may be reproduced in any form without written permission from the publisher.

While every care has been taken to ensure the accuracy of the information in this guide, time brings change, and consequently, the publisher cannot accept responsibility for errors that may occur. Call ahead to verify prices and other information.

First Edition
ISBN 0-679-00799-7
ISSN 1535-5047

Special Sales

Fodor's Travel Publications are available at special discounts for bulk purchases for sales promotions or premiums. Special editions, including personalized covers, excerpts of existing guides, and corporate imprints, can be created in large quantities for special needs. For more information, contact your local bookseller or write to Special Markets, Fodor's Travel Publications, 280 Park Ave., New York, NY 10017. Inquiries from Canada should be directed to your local Canadian bookseller or sent to Random House of Canada, Ltd., Marketing Dept., 2775 Matheson Boulevard East, Mississauga, Ontario L4W 4P7. Inquiries from the United Kingdom should be sent to Fodor's Travel Publications, 20 Vauxhall Bridge Road, London, England SW1V 2SA.

PRINTED IN GERMANY
10 9 8 7 6 5 4 3 2 1

Library of Congress Cataloging-in-Publication Data available upon request.

Acknowledgments

Catherine Karnow gives sincere thanks to Whitney Brewer at Southwest Airlines, and to David Lansing, who has become a new friend. I owe a special debt to Fabrizio La Rocca, whose intellectual curiosity, appreciation of my anecdotes, and amusement at my mishaps added excitement to my desert journeys. I must also express my admiration for the brilliant way he and Tigist Getachew designed the book.

From David Lansing: My thanks to Fabrizio, who continued to pull me back from the brink when I was ready to join the desert lemmings and jump off some Anza-Borrego cliff; and to Catherine, whose sharp eye gave me insights into a world I sometimes didn't see; but mostly to Michelle Nicolosi, who provided invaluable support on this project. The stories in this book wouldn't be possible without the characters who make the American desert such a magnet for eccentrics: Eagle Feather, L'Dona, Uqualla, Gib, Borrego Paul, Nolan Clay, Riff Markowitz, and Steve Wynn, just to name a few. And where would I have hung my hat if not for Sheila Donnelly Theroux, Babs Harrison, Tracy Conrad, Deb Bridges, and many more. And thanks to Jan and Paige, two ocean girls who patiently endured this desert rat.

Credits

Creative Director and Series Editor: Fabrizio La Rocca
Editorial Director: Karen Cure
Art Director: Tigist Getachew

Editor: Candice Gianetti
Editorial Assistant: Dennis Sarlo
Production/Manufacturing: C. R. Bloodgood, Robert B. Shields
Maps: David Lindroth, Inc.

Other Escape Guides

Escape to the Amalfi Coast • Escape to the Hawaiian Islands
Escape to Ireland • Escape to Morocco • Escape to Provence
Escape to the Riviera • Escape to Tuscany
Available in bookstores

Most books on the travel shelves are either long on the nitty-gritty and short on evocative photographs, or the other way around. We at Fodor's think that the different balance in this slim volume is just perfect, rather like the intersection of the most luscious magazine article and a sensible, down-to-earth guidebook. On the road, the useful pages at the end of the book are practically all you need. For the planning, roam through the stories and the photographs up front: Each one reveals a key facet of the vast and variegated desert that fills the southwestern corner of the United States, and conveys a sense of place that will take you there before you go. Each page opens up to exceptional experiences; each spread leads you to the spirit of the American desert at its purest.

Some of these places are sure to beckon. You may yearn to discover a desert of endless dunes and brilliant skies—a desert of almost unimaginable aridity—or to canter across a dusty canyon like the Duke in a John Ford film. You may consider journeying to the heart of the Navajo nation, to an Apache rodeo, or to Arizona's Frank Lloyd Wright desert landmarks. You can experience a sandstorm, explore a ghost town, lose a hundred bucks in the shadow of a faux Eiffel Tower, or tune up your chakras and adjust your aura in Sedona. Then end the day on a desert bluff watching the pink-and-orange sunset light show, or seek refuge in the bungalow complex where Clark Gable and Carole Lombard honeymooned.

It was the extraordinary people of the desert who drew the attention of author David Lansing and photographer Catherine Karnow. Lansing has long come to the desert in search of solitude. Photojournalist Karnow, who initially hesitated to embark on a project involving (as she thought) "vast spaces of nothing," was soon captivated by the light of White Sands—always changing and always dramatic—and she found herself drawn back day after day, even to the same dunes. The desert excited Karnow's sense of the unusual, and the photographs in this book reveal her fascination with the exquisitely beautiful, and unexpected, signs of life in these American landscapes.

It has happened to centuries of travelers before her, and it will happen to you. So forget your projects and deadlines. And escape to the American Desert. You owe it to yourself.

—The Editors

AN HOUR AGO THE SKY WAS THE COLOR OF BLEACHED DENIM, the dunes so glaringly white in the staggering heat that even with hat and sunglasses you squinted as you trudged along an unmarked trail through this vastness of powdery gypsum sand. Don't get lost, you reminded yourself, pausing frequently to make sure Gardner Peak, in the distant San Andreas Mountains to the west, was still where it should be. Perhaps it was the softening of the September light or the almost indiscernible metallic smell in the faint breeze that first alerted you to a change in the weather. Now wispy mare's-tail clouds darken ominously in the southwest. The wind picks up, blowing grains of sand against your ankles and legs. A thunderstorm is approaching. Time to turn around and follow your

A Storm on the Sand Sea

WHITE SANDS NATIONAL MONUMENT, ALAMOGORDO, NM

Sink up to your ankles or take a dry bath in the powdery white gypsum sand. The undulating dunes stretch off into the horizon.

solitary tracks back through the barren interdunes that twist and turn through a maze of towering sand hills 50 feet high. Quickly, before the rain washes away any trace of your passing. The shadows from the nearing storm cast a cool blue light across the dunes, transforming them into a pitching ocean. What once looked eternally still and solid now seems as fluid as a rolling breaker. Though black masses of clouds have blocked your view of the westerly mountains, you're certain you're heading in the right direction. You remember passing that skunkbush sumac, wrapped in a mounded plaster cast of gypsum, on your way in. And there are the three brittle soaptree yuccas where you first stopped to drink some water. As a thunderclap rends the desert silence and a whip of pure electricity cracks the endless sky, you see the glint of your car in the deserted parking lot and take refuge just as the first large drops of rain plop against your chalky windshield. You made it.

Life, in the form of earless lizards and sky-pointing yuccas, thrives even in this beautiful but harsh environment where adaptation is an art.

Everything is shaped by the elements:
rain leeching gypsum from the surrounding
hills, wind depositing it in mounds,
even lightning, which can fuse large
clumps of sand into desert glass.

OLD MEN IN BUCKSKIN ROBES CHANT AND TELL STORIES WHILE YOUNG MEN IN faded jeans show off their roping skills, but what's brought you to this sparsely populated mesa is the women. Dressed in bright velour dresses, they sit straight-backed before vertical looms, silently weaving the colors of the desert into beautiful geometric designs in wool, careful to leave a "spirit trail"—a line of yarn running through the outer edge that, they say, keeps the weaver's creative energies from being trapped inside the rug. A vintage piece up for auction today is similar to one a woman is at work on. Stop for a moment to watch, and she smiles. She tells you her name is Evelyn Curley, that her father built her first loom in 1935, when she was eight, and her mother taught her how to weave this design, as she has taught her five daughters. The Ganado Red—an elaborate pattern of black and gray zigzags, crosses,

The Spirit Trail

HUBBELL TRADING POST, NAVAJO NATION, AZ

Some Navajo artisans still raise the sheep, shear the wool, and make dyes from native plants for the threads they weave on their vertical looms. Patterns evolve over time.

and elongated diamonds on a soft red background—is Evelyn's favorite because of its complexity and because, she tells you, "it was a favorite of Don Lorenzo." That is how the Navajo still refer to John Lorenzo Hubbell, the legendary dean of Southwest traders, who established this post on the reservation in 1878 and helped the tribe's skilled weavers develop what was then a more utilitarian craft into the prized art it is today. The long stone trading post is much as it was a hundred years ago, when Navajo, Hopi, and Zuni Indians came from all around the Four Corners to swap their colorful rugs, intricate baskets, delicate pottery, and exquisite silver jewelry for goods like flour, canned food, calico, and saddles. They trade here still. "Go inside and look," Evelyn says. "Nothing's changed. Only the names of the weavers."

A four- by six-foot rug requires three months of a master weaver's life and may fetch $7,500 or more, but fewer and fewer young women have the patience or the inclination to take up the art of their grandmothers. Soon these textile sculptures may be extinct.

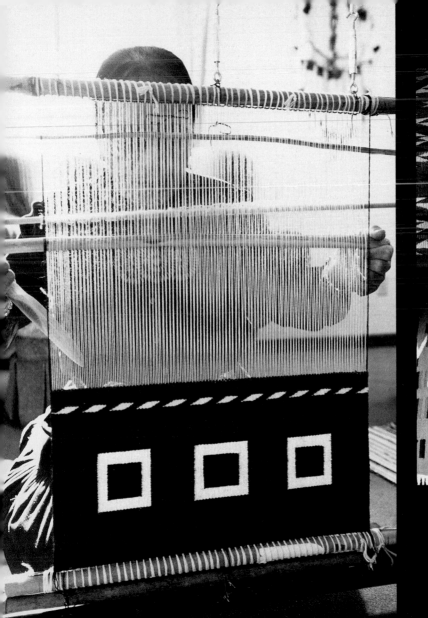

IT'S NOT UNTIL THE SECOND DAY OUT THAT YOU THINK ABOUT THAT little disclaimer at the bottom of the form the outfitter had you sign: "Changes may occur due to weather or other unexpected events." These are phrases concocted by skittish lawyers in the outside world, but down here, in this long, flat canyon where the air has turned red from a sudden sandstorm, it's just the way things are. "Hold tight to your horse's reins," the guide yells through the howling storm that blasts you and your trembling chestnut, named Duke after the actor who, with John Ford, made this valley instantly recognizable in films like *Stagecoach* and *She Wore a Yellow Ribbon*. Stinging grains of sand and bruising clumps of dirt pelt you, and it's impossible to see where you're going, but you do your best to keep Duke's nose just

Riding with the Duke

ON HORSEBACK THROUGH MONUMENT VALLEY, AZ/UT

Mesas tower, the desert ripples, and the cobalt-blue sky, flecked with wispy white clouds, stretches endlessly above you. No wonder filmmakers love it here.

inches from the tail of the horse in front of you as your guide navigates an invisible trail through purple sage and yellow prickly pear. After 15 or 20 minutes, you're on the other side of the canyon, hunkered down behind a rock outcropping that shields you from the wind until the storm passes. Soon the sky clears, unveiling a wondrous twilight view of the Mittens rock formation. "I know I said we'd make it a little further today," says your guide, dismounting, "but I think we'll just maybe make camp here tonight. Unless anyone objects." No one does. As the color of the sky shifts from rust to royal blue, you drink up the vista of the great buttes and mesas before you while Duke, God bless him, takes his modest reward: warm water in a canvas bucket.

Rugged, wind-parched wilderness is best seen
on horseback. There's just something about
a long ride followed by a blazing campfire
and a hearty meal, prepared in Dutch ovens
and soot-covered cast-iron skillets.

Into the Vortex

SEDONA, AZ

ESCAPE TO THE AMERICAN DESERT

SINCE LONG BEFORE A 1980S PSYCHIC DISCOVERED SEDONA'S MYSTERIOUS "VORTICES"—PLACES where the spectacular iron-red rock formations are said to emit swirling pools of spirit-charging energy—Boynton Canyon has been a sacred place to the local tribes. Fitting, then, that your guide for a walk up the canyon is a Havasupai Indian named Uqualla, concierge at the Enchantment Resort, which not only is protected by a pillar of rocks known as Kachina Woman but butts right up against a vortex. Dressed in a turquoise tunic and white deerskin boots, Uqualla leads the way while telling stories about how Spider Woman gave power to Sedona's red earth. Later, your masseuse, who moved to this New Age mecca from Maine 10 years ago because she had a dream in which a man who looked like Julio Iglesias told her she should, gives her own interpretation of the secrets of Sedona. Placing crystals at chakra points on your body, she anoints you with oils from holy places—Tibet, Machu

Eagle Feather's hair is braided
with a brass bell at the end, used
to call the angels when he gives
tarot readings.

Picchu, the Egyptian pyramids—while invoking a wide range of gods, saints, and spirits to bring you peace and open your heart in a ceremony she calls the Awakening. Palms of her hands on the soles of your feet, she chants a mantra before imploring Mother Earth to cleanse your aura. Or get your aura and chakra tune-ups, along with a vortex map, at the Center for the New Age, a sort of psychic mini-mall where you can stock up on healing stones like black coral to absorb negativity, a copper pyramid you wear on your head, Tibetan singing bowls to invoke a hypnotic state, Good Karma yo-yos, power bracelets, problem-solving candles . . . there's even a room full of nothing but crystals. Take your pick. It's all good.

SPILLING DOWN THE LOW SLOPE OF A MESA, ITS SHAPES ECHOING the raw sawtooth hills at its back, Taliesin West is so suited to the Sonoran Desert that it looks as if it grew slowly out of the sandy soil like the surrounding saguaros. In a way, it did. Called to Arizona to help design the Phoenix Biltmore, Frank Lloyd Wright found inspiration in the desert landscape; he came up with an iconographic geometric pattern for the hotel after studying nature's design on the trunk of a tree. In 1937 he began building his winter home, studio, and school on 600 acres in the foothills of the nearby McDowell Mountains, and he kept refining and redefining it until his death in 1959. Back then it was a difficult, long drive from the city across a dusty riverbed, but if you and your car survived the journey, the eccentric architect warmly welcomed you. This

An Architect of Nature

FINDING FRANK LLOYD WRIGHT IN THE ARIZONA DESERT

Taliesen is a child of its dramatic setting. Rocks from the hills and sand from the washes were used to build this masterpiece of light and shadow, geometry and poetry.

morning it's a short jaunt down the freeway, yet the astonishment you feel when you first catch sight of the bold design—a testament to Wright's belief in an "organic" architecture in harmony with its environment—is the same. Walk up the gravel path, beneath the vine-covered pergola, to his workroom, its long, sloping walls built from rocks and sand scooped up out of the desert. In the Garden Room, sit for a moment in chairs he designed and feel how the space, filled with light filtered through its sloping translucent ceiling, seems perfectly linked to its setting by the room's expansive windows. "My view from here," wrote the architect, is "a look over the rim of the world." Today your view is the same.

Frolic early, swim late. In between, pull the shades against the glaring midday sun and nap, or lounge indulgently over lunch as the Biltmore's crisply dressed waiters pour glasses of minted iced tea.

A YOUNG COWBOY IN A BLACK FELT HAT TAPES UP A BUSTED hand while waiting his turn. His name is Vincent Shorty, and he gives it a go on a vicious bull named Pistol Pete. He doesn't quite last the required eight seconds, and when he lands hard on the dusty red earth, it takes him a few minutes to catch his breath and stand up. The other cowboys, all banged up as well, have names like Julyan Yellowhair, Cody Boozer, and Wilford Peaches. They ride bulls named No Excuse, Nothing Matters, and Gizmo. Gizmo, in particular, is one tough animal, and all the cowboys shake their heads in nervous anticipation when the gate opens and the bull explodes sideways, quickly sending its rider to the ground, where he is stomped on by 2,000 pounds of angry bovine. The crowd's pretty used to such things by now, of course—there have

An Apache Rodeo

WHITERIVER, WHITE MOUNTAIN APACHE RESERVATION, AZ

Riding bad-tempered bulls is a young man's game. Older hands check equipment, make sure the gates work properly, and draw the beasts' attention as rodeo clowns.

been rodeos here in Whiteriver for more than 75 years, the big Labor Day one attracting more than 800 Native Americans from the United States and Canada hoping to bull-ride, barrel-race, steer-wrestle, and rope their way to glory. While the medical team tends to the downed cowboy, Nolan Clay, who's running this spring show, encourages everyone to take a break and visit the snack bar. "That Indian fry bread smells so good, don't it?" he cajoles. "I'll tell you what, if anyone could ever invent a cologne that smelled like it, he'd make a fortune." A little girl with a blue sash across her chest that says MISS RODEO APACHE L'IL BIT tries to calm her horse, spooked by the wind, by riding in tight circles outside the bull pens. "You ready, L'il Bit?" Nolan asks. She nods and gallops into the ring, smiling and waving at the crowd, a regal Indian princess.

Indian rodeos reflect the hard living and stoic culture of the participants. Crowds are quiet and respectful. Winners and losers disdain showboating—first prize is accepted with a nod of the head.

The Secrets of Life

THE LIVING DESERT, PALM DESERT, CA

A SPRIGHTLY OLD MAN IN DR. LIVINGSTON GARB—PITH HELMET, SWEATY BANDANNA AROUND HIS neck, khaki shirt and pants—crumbles a grayish-green leaf in his hand and bids you to smell it. "Desert lavender," he says, "the most fragrant plant in our garden." "Our garden" is a preserve called the Living Desert. Here 10 ecosystem habitats showcase the astonishing array of plants and animals that thrive where rainfall can average less than five inches a year and the sun can be blistering. Though the heat is quite bearable this April morning in the shade of the lush Palm Oasis, a minute ago, in the Upper Colorado Garden, with its prickly chollas and scarlet-flowered ocotillos, it seemed easily over a hundred degrees. The ground temperature, the docent explains, is 130 right now, but a few inches below it's just 72. That's one of the secrets of life in the desert, he says. It's how kangaroo rats and banded geckos, kit foxes and fringe-toed lizards, avoid the debilitating heat: They sleep underground.

Dry, hot, and hostile, yes, but the desert is not a wasteland. Flowers bloom, predators hunt, and life goes on.

Lucky for you, not every creature here is nocturnal. Gambel's quail coo beneath a blue paloverde tree while two roadrunners, their speckled wings spread wide like a matador's cape, thread through patches of goldenhead flowers and hedgehog cacti in search of beetles, scorpions, even small snakes. Overhead, dry fan-palm leaves rustle where orioles search out the sweet, datelike seeds. Once this area had dozens of dense groves of fan palms, the man tells you; the palms grew around springs or seeps, but as the groundwater was pumped out to support golf courses and vast resorts, the groves died off. "These are some of the last of 'em," he says, gently patting a trunk. "I hope they live longer than I do, but I don't know. I just don't know."

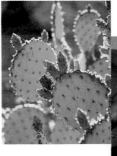

THERE WAS A TIME, BACK IN THE '40S AND '50S, WHEN DISAPPEARING to Palm Springs meant you were going to be a little wicked. That's why the stars went there: to get away from the glare of Hollywood lights and the eyes of snoopy reporters. In the desert you could drink martinis all night at the Racquet Club, where Bing Crosby liked to play bartender, and later—much later—follow the laughter to the pool, where starlets like Marilyn Monroe skinny-dipped until the darkness gave way to the dawn. Muffled jazz spilled out of private bungalows, and partygoers—famous directors, writers, singers—stumbled out into the night, trying to remember their way home. They were all here: Gloria Swanson, Spencer Tracy, Cary Grant. Black-and-white photos in the lobby of the club's Bamboo Bar show them playing tennis or

Desert Babylon

STARRY NIGHTS IN PALM SPRINGS, CA

Sex springs eternal in this oasis where sexagenarians strut their stuff to "A Pretty Girl Is Like a Melody" and passion blooms like blood-red bougainvillea on white stucco walls.

chess or just lounging by the pool, but that was during the sunbaked days. It was after dark, when the warm, jasmine-scented air was as alluring as a Mae West come-on, that the real games began. Today stars still gather poolside at chic retreats like the Moroccan fantasy Korakia and the Willows, where Clark Gable and Carole Lombard honeymooned. Some seem like they've never left: They're performing in the Fabulous Palm Springs Follies at the Plaza Theatre, where Jack Benny broadcast his live radio show in the '30s. Impresario Riff Markowitz, dapper in a white tux, introduces a chorus line of long-legged beauties in feathers and sequins, as well as torch singers, tap dancers, and naughty comedians—not one under the age of 55. It takes you back. To a time when the desert was a private refuge for stars, a place to get away from it all and, perhaps, be a little wicked.

Blue pools of martinis, elegantly thin palm trees, and luxurious inns with evocative names—the Willows, Korakia, the Orchid Tree—remind you why stars like Frank Sinatra and Joan Crawford came here in the first place.

THE PONYTAILED GUIDE STOPS THE JEEP IN THE MIDDLE OF A SANDY wash that doubles as the road to Font's Point and the undisputed best panoramic view of the Borrego Badlands. "Listen," he says, cocking his head. "Hear it?" In the late-afternoon stillness the only noise you hear is the popping of the cooling engine and the sound of your own breath. "There's a river beneath us," says the guide. "If you can keep your mind still long enough, you'll hear it." Hopping out of the Jeep, Borrego Paul leads you up a gray bluff high above a landscape marked by hundreds of weather-worn hills twisting in all directions, as if there'd been a cataclysmic crash of uplifting continental plates right in the middle of the desert. Stark and treeless, they absorb the dark shadows and radiate muted earth tones, mimicking the sky, which is layered

Sounding an Ancient Sea

ANZA-BORREGO DESERT STATE PARK, BORREGO SPRINGS, CA

What would the bottom of the ocean look like if the waters suddenly retreated? Stand at the crumbling edge of Font's Point and see for yourself.

like a parfait in hues from washed-out blue to glowing orange to sated purple. "This was once all under the sea," Paul whispers. A forgotten, ancient ocean. Great whales and manta rays with hundred-foot wingspans glided over what is now the desert floor. In these hills are prehistoric shells and shark teeth and the rib bones of leviathans. Sit on the bluff at dusk and watch the light slowly change colors. The rutted hills, carved by a million years of violent rainstorms and scouring winds, grow moody in the dusk. Be still. Listen hard. Then, when the darkness envelops you, slowly tiptoe away, head bowed in silence, listening to the murmur of an ancient sea.

AGAVE →
FERN →
YUCCA →
DESERT STAR →
LOCUST →
LUPINE →
MARIGOLD →
MESQUITE →
POPPY →
SMOKE TREE →

Wildflowers, as rare in the
Badlands as the desert sheep that
give Anza-Borrego half its name,
pop up as trailheads. Jeeps
explore nameless gulches and
numbered roads leading nowhere.

EVEN IN THE SEARING HEAT HE LOOKS DAPPER, THOUGH THE wardrobe is outdated: wool trousers, yellow-and-black-checked sport coat, stiff white shirt buttoned to the top. He seems nervous, flitting around the pool, a bit lost. "Who is that guy?" you ask the cocktail waitress in pink shorts and halter top. But when she looks up, he is gone. "Must have been Ben," she says, handing you an umbrella-shaded drink. "People see him around here all the time." Benjamin "Bugsy" Siegel has been dead for 50 years, of course, but his harried spirit still keeps an eye on the town he helped create. They say he was spotted in the gutted casino of the Dunes the night they blew it up to make way for the dancing fountains and Tuscan villas of the Bellagio's faux Lake Como, and again in front of the Sands

City of Illusion

EUROPEAN ESCAPES IN LAS VEGAS, NV

The Vegas mirage: The faux Paris Opera is less crowded, Lake Como more serene, and the shrunken Eiffel Tower more majestic against an azure desert sky.

when it fell to make room for the Venetian. Why not? Vegas has always been about illusion and fantasy, whether it was wiseguys opening oasis-themed parlors of vice in the '50s or today's ultimate surrealistic hallucinations that conjure Europe in the middle of the American desert. Rub your eyes hard before the Paris casino's Arc de Triomphe or its half-scale Eiffel Tower, whose wrought-iron legs hum an eerie tune when the gritty desert winds blow. Pinch yourself to see if you're dreaming as a gondolier poles you under an arched bridge on the Grand Canal where Casanovas sing Italian love songs. Feeling every bit as confused as Bugsy's apparition, you wander into a wax museum on St. Mark's Square, where other Vegas legends suddenly appear: a Rat Pack–era Sinatra, hat cocked to the side, and Elvis in his signature white jumpsuit blazing with rhinestones. Like Bugsy, they may have left the building, but they have never left mythical Vegas.

Sin City has evolved into a desert Disneyland. Tiffany and Gucci boutiques, Cirque du Soleil and pirate shows, and outposts of haut chefs like Wolfgang Puck and Emeril Lagasse have replaced the sex shops, nude chorus girls, and dirt-cheap all-you-can-eat buffets of yore.

47

SNOW FLURRIES SWIRL IN A BITTER WIND THAT SWEEPS AWAY THE SOUNDS OF modern life, transporting you back a hundred, three hundred, even a thousand years. The smell of juniper smoke from unseen chimneys is thick in the canyon. Stop the horses for a moment along the shallow, muddy wash, and listen to the tinkling of sheep bells and the caw of a crow floating in the thermals of the sheer thousand-foot red-sandstone walls. Your piebald horse nervously whinnies, and you hear what sounds like the cry of a faraway baby. "Just the wind," says your Navajo guide. "It's a trickster, like Coyote." His family has lived in this canyon, amid hundreds of ruins of their vanished predecessors, the Anasazi, "since the time of the Long Walk." As you meander past the barren cottonwoods and tamarisks, he tells stories of ancient days when Grandmother Spider taught the Navajo to weave. "Do you know about the tomb

Listen to the Wind

CANYON DE CHELLY, CHINLE, AZ

In this wonderland of rock, snow softens visual landmarks and sharpens auditory memories. A sense of peace descends.

of the weaver?" he asks, then points across the canyon to the north rim. Some archaeologists were digging around back in the '20s, he says, when they came across a tomb in an alcove in the rock about 50 feet above the canyon. In it was the well-preserved body of an old man, wrapped in a blanket made mostly of the feathers of golden eagles. Beneath that blanket was another of white cotton, in perfect condition, and over the feathers were a spindle and more than two miles of cotton yarn coiled in skeins. Some say the old man was a master weaver, your guide tells you, "but others know he was the son of Grandmother Spider." Ride on slowly, listening to the wind, the sheep bells, and the stories told by the canyon.

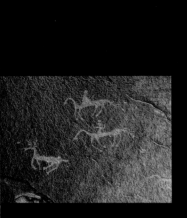

This canyon is a spiritual place for the Navajo, who believe it to be the heart of the world. Their tribal ancestress Spider Woman is said to live at the top of Spider Rock—a monolith that rises 800 feet straight up from the canyon floor—surrounded by the bones of naughty children.

THERE IS SOMETHING ABOUT SAGUAROS THAT FASCINATES. PERHAPS it is their too-human shape, some arms upraised as in perpetual if prickly welcome while others bend and twist, giving each cactus a distinct personality. To see them, head for the Sonoran Desert, a surprisingly lush and diverse landscape that is their only natural habitat. Driving west out of Tucson, pull in at an overlook at the top of Gates Pass and step under a shady ramada to savor the panorama. Framed between ragged fringes of mountains far to the north and southwest lie miles and miles of desert dominated by these magnificent cacti. To get closer, walk the trails at Saguaro National Park in the early morning, when all the textures of the desert washed out in the intensity of the noonday sun are revealed. Towering above the

The Old Man of the Desert

SAGUARO NATIONAL PARK, TUCSON, AZ

Saguaros start life as tiny black seeds that germinate in the shelter of nurse plants like paloverdes and mesquite. Seventy-five years later the first arms will sprout.

mesquite and ocotillos, the prickly pears and chollas, are the saguaros. Each stands sentinel over its patch of sandy soil, providing sustenance through its big, bold flowers to whitewing doves and long-nose bats while harboring warblers and other nesting birds in holes woodpeckers have chiseled out of its trunk and arms. Later, driving slowly along the park's mostly dirt roads, you stop again and again to admire these regal plants and have your picture taken beside them. Solemn and serene, like a cactus buddha, the giant next to you—reaching as high as a four-story building from its start as a seed the size of a pinhead—may be two centuries old. Through all that time, through the lightning, turbulent winds, and severe droughts, through blazing heat and freezing cold, the saguaro has endured. He has earned your admiration. For he truly is the old man of the desert.

The saguaro is the classic emblem of the Old West—so much so that in the Jimmy Stewart western *Broken Arrow* plaster-of-paris stand-ins were planted among the red rocks of Sedona in cinematic defiance of reality.

YOUR NEWFOUND FRIENDS INTRODUCE THEMSELVES AS ZELDA and Goathead. "Goathead isn't his real name," Zelda says. "That's just what I call him because he always gets flats." Zelda, with a toothy grin and wraparound mirror sunglasses, notices your confusion and explains: "Goatheads are the nasty little bumps. Best to avoid them." The two drove all night from Colorado to reach Moab, whose red-rock cliffs have attracted adventurers since Butch Cassidy's Wild Bunch hung out here. Like you, the pair has come to tackle the most famous trail in this mountain biker's mecca, Slickrock. Now you're standing at the head of a 2-mile practice loop, wondering if you're really up to this. "It's no sweat," Zelda says comfortingly. "I took it last summer

Zoom Zoom Zoom

SLICKROCK MOUNTAIN-BIKE TRAIL, MOAB, UT

The trick to easy riding is to take advantage of the unbelievably high-traction sandstone. And keep your pedals centered.

and only got two kisses"—the raw strawberry patches where your legs scrape against the rough sandstone when you tumble off your bike. You hear Moab has tougher trails, where some of the best bikers in the world try their luck at impossible climbs, amazing leaps, and wicked turns, but right now this practice loop seems plenty steep and treacherous as it swoops and climbs over rocks that look like sleeping elephants. As you bottom out in one hair-raising dip, your pedal digs into the bronze rock and you swerve and slide, heart pounding, but somehow manage to avoid a fall. Zelda sips from her plastic water bottle and waits for you to catch your breath. Your legs are shaking, and your entire body feels jittery from the adrenaline. Perhaps you should just ride back to the trailhead. "Look at that desert view," Zelda says, admiring the craggy outcroppings that look as if they belong on Mars. "Makes it all worthwhile, doesn't it?" It does, you decide, climbing back on your bike and following her down the trail.

Wheeling through this
landscape that feels
prehistoric, or perhaps
extraterrestrial, you find
yourself again and again
stopping dead in your
tracks to drink it all in, or
perching on a weather-
carved roost to contemplate
the meaning of life.

THOUGH MOST SEATS IN THE AMARGOSA OPERA HOUSE ARE EMPTY tonight, the theater seems warm, inviting, full of life. Perhaps it's the golden-haired cherubs frolicking in a blue-sky mural on the ceiling or the fan-waving Spanish noblewomen leaning over the trompe-l'oeil balcony. The Gypsies, bullfighters, and nuns painted on the walls give solace to ballerina Marta Becket on nights like this as she twirls like a dust devil to music by Strauss and Tchaikovsky. That's why she created them—in the heat and isolation of the Mojave, you won't always play to a packed house. Fifty years ago Marta danced on Broadway and at Radio City Music Hall, but in 1967 she found her true calling: dancing in the desert. After the show, as the lithe septuagenarian signs a glossy photo of herself in a pink tutu, you express your

Desert Eccentrics

AN OPERA HOUSE AND A CASTLE NEAR DEATH VALLEY, CA

If there is no audience, you simply paint one. Besides, what else is a creative soul to do while waiting for the magic of the night?

admiration for what was anything but an ordinary performance. She fixes you with her dark brown eyes. "I would never want to be ordinary," she says. Death Valley Scotty must have felt the same way. It's a shame the two never met—he'd passed on by the time serendipity brought Marta to the dilapidated old hotel she transformed into an opera house. Surely the two would have understood each other perfectly. Scotty, once a cowboy with Buffalo Bill Cody's Wild West Show, was a huckster, or so you're told as you poke around Scotty's Castle, 50 miles north of Amargosa in Death Valley National Park. There's gold in these hills, he convinced his benefactor Albert Johnson, a Chicago millionaire, who built this Moorish fantasy—later a hotel drawing the likes of Betty Grable and Will Rogers—for visits with his wife while Scotty supposedly mined. He never did strike gold, except in his friendship with Johnson and in their love of the desert. Perhaps that was enough.

To Marta Becket, all the world's a stage. The empty town dissolves around her; the desert doyenne dances on.

Tall tales swirl about the castle named for Death Valley Scotty—most of which he invented himself. Was he a huckster or a millionaire? Was the mansion ever really his? The answers are buried with him on a hill overlooking this grand desert folly.

LAST NIGHT, UNABLE TO SLEEP, YOU LAY IN BED LISTENING TO THE hissing sprinklers fed by spring water from the deep blue pool at Furnace Creek. Now, an hour after sunrise, you sit at the edge of the refilled pool and watch a young woman in a red bathing suit floating on her back. She notices you out of the corner of her eye, smiles, and says, "Why is it a pool feels so sinful in the desert?" In Death Valley, it's because water means life. The landscape around you is a passion play, with nature's redeemer, water, in the starring role. Consider the amazing landforms around you and the names early explorers attached to them: Saline Valley, Deadman's Pass, Last Chance Mountain. Death Valley. When you climb out of your air-conditioned car at Badwater, the lowest, hottest, driest point in North America, the

Outer Limits

DEATH VALLEY NATIONAL PARK, CA

Every other night the spring-fed pool at Furnace Creek is emptied to irrigate the surrounding golf course. The inland sea over Badwater emptied long ago.

first thing you notice is that the air has texture. Like a heavy blanket draped over your head. The second thing you notice, amid the blinding whiteness, is the smell of the tan-colored spring-fed pool. Like liquid sulfur. Legend has it that it's poisonous, but you defy the myth by scooping up a shallow handful and swirling it in your mouth. It tastes metallic, sickening, like Epsom-salt soup. Badwater seems the perfect name for this nonredemptive spring. As Devil's Golf Course does for the surrounding salt flats that extend for miles into the heat-wave-warped horizon. Tens of thousands of years ago, where you are standing was a lake 600 feet deep and 100 miles long. Now it is 200 square miles of crystallized-mineral crust pocked with jagged little hillocks of desiccated salts. Bones of a lost lake, gnarled corpse of a vanquished savior.

Water—its presence
or absence—defines
Death Valley. Hemmed
in by nine mountain
ranges, it is one
of the driest, hottest
places on earth.

MILES FROM NOWHERE, ON A STARK STRETCH OF HIGH DESERT, SITS THE HUSK OF what was once a boomtown. So fierce is the weather that only a lure as powerful as gold could have built a town here. Once that ran out, there was no reason on earth or under it to hang around. Walk the deserted streets, past the jail, a gambling house, a couple of the 60 or so saloons and dance halls that thrived in Bodie's heyday, and your imagination stirs with stories of the town whose reputation for lawlessness spawned the phrase "Goodbye, God. I'm going to Bodie." The Miner's Union Hall is a modest museum now, filled with the detritus of abandoned lives: a silver baby spoon, a yellowed ivory comb, cracked leather boots. There are several old handguns as well— guns like the one that killed the Cornish miner Thomas Treloar here on a bitter-cold January night in 1881. Picture a spirited group of miners and their wives spinning

Queen of the Ghost Towns

BODIE STATE HISTORIC PARK, NEAR BRIDGEPORT, CA

In this forsaken, lonely place, every plank of worn wood, every dusty miner's pick and shop window, has a story to tell.

round and round as fiddlers work up a crowd made up mostly of single men like the ne'er-do-well Frenchman Joseph DeRoche. Fueled by cheap whiskey and a woman with eyes greener than emeralds, he drags Treloar's wife onto the dance floor, much against her wishes. When the two men step outside to settle their differences, DeRoche pulls out a pistol and shoots Treloar in the head. Lynched for his crime, DeRoche is buried in Boot Hill with other outcasts like Tom Dillon, a crazed opium addict, and ladies of the night like Rosa May, a pretty Irish girl gone wrong, and Eleanor Dumont, known as Madame Mustache for the obvious reason. When the wind whistles through the wooden skeletons of the town, you can almost hear the ghosts of those who said goodbye to God and died in Bodie.

A coupe's rusted carcass, tattered curtains stitched by hands long still, a weedy grave plot: modern petroglyphs waiting to be interpreted, tales ready to unfold.

FROM LAS CRUCES, THE TWO-LANE COUNTRY ROAD MEANDERS north through dense orchards of pecan trees and row after row of shiny green plants bowed from the weight of glistening pods of varying sizes and colors: chiles, the pride of New Mexico. Pungent whiffs of smoke wafting through the Rincon Valley draw you to the little town of Hatch, where a billboard beside a stucco building dressed up in bright red *ristras*—fat strings of peppers hung to dry from windows, doorways, and roofs everywhere you look—welcomes you to the Hatch Chile Festival. Out at the fairgrounds, last year's Chile Festival Queen sits on a folding chair, munching a smoked turkey leg, while Gib, the mayor, announces the contestants in the fiddle contest. The playing is lively, the beat sturdy and sure, and several campesinos put down their plates of gorditas or sweet

A Pandemonium of Peppers

HATCH CHILE FESTIVAL, HATCH, NM

Your brow sweats, your eyes tear, and— if they're *really* good— they can take your breath away. To true Chileheads, eating fire's worth all the pain.

tamales to hoof it out on the dance floor with their wives and girlfriends. It's sweltering beneath the aluminum roof of the open-sided exhibition hall on this Labor Day weekend, but it's even hotter outside, where local farmers rack up sales from pickups stacked high with 40-pound sacks of fiery habaneros, famous Hatch greens, and other red, yellow, and orange chiles. For a few bucks more, they'll roast them for you in mesh drums spun over butane fires—source, apparently, of those first smoky come-ons. Load up at booths hawking every kind of dish that can be made with chiles, then dig in while you watch young *folklorico* dancers twirl their rainbow-colored skirts as they stomp their feet and clap their hands in celebration. It's harvest time in the Chile Capital of the World.

First planted along the Rio Grande by
the Spanish, embraced by the Pueblo natives,
and adopted by Anglos, chiles today have
a multicultural following that's reflected in
those who gather in Hatch to celebrate
them—in dance, in music, and in the art
of cleverly strung ristras.

All the Details

You're lying on your back atop an immense sandstone snake frozen in place millions of years ago. They tell you it's a sand dune, but you can't shake the feeling that it is somehow alive—or waiting to be. These sinewy "dunes" of Moab's desert surround you, frozen in midmigration, as if at any moment they will resume their journey across the vast sands. It is night. You are alone. You watch the stars travel across the sky, study the smoke of your breath. You pace your dune creature from head to tail, sit on his head and give him a name. Let's go, you whisper. What are you waiting for? You should sleep, you think, but then maybe not, for this is why you came to the desert: to sit up all night with the stars, to pace frozen dunes, to see what the world sounds like when no one is talking.

The solitude and otherworldly beauty of the North American deserts draw people looking to get away, find themselves, find something else. But that same remoteness can make getting to the desert something of a chore. Many of the adventures in this book are off the beaten track—don't expect to find an airport within 15 minutes, and don't expect four-star accommodations or fine dining. But logging miles in a trek across long stretches of emptiness between cities is part of what discovering the desert is all about. So get in a Zen mood, and get ready to drive.

Three of the four major North American deserts—the Mojave, the Sonoran, and the Chihuahuan—are called "hot" deserts, and do get unbearably hot during the long summer. Farther north is the "cold" Great Basin Desert, higher in elevation and much cooler, with often harsh and snowy winters. The following section, which gives the nitty-gritty on each of our escapes, is organized geographically, as your travels are likely to be. Wherever you go, be sure to stick to the basic safety rules of the desert: when exploring on foot, always carry one gallon of water per person per day. Take seriously the usual sun precautions; always wear sunscreen, and bring a hat. Don't stray from the beaten paths—it's easy to get lost in the desert, and not so easy to find your way out. If your car dies, stay with it; experts say it's easier to find a car than a person. Four-wheel-drive vehicles are helpful on dirt roads, and get you into some spectacular backcountry areas. (For more tips on desert driving, see www.caldrive.com/desert.html.) Weather can change fast; to avoid surprise monsoons, windstorms, and snow, call ahead; and to be ready for scorching days that become chilly evenings, dress in layers. Most parks are closed on Christmas and some on Thanksgiving. Unless otherwise stated, accommodations are open year-round, accept credit cards, and have all private-bath rooms.

The following are the tourism offices for the states covered in this book: AZ: Office of Tourism, 2702 N. 3rd St., Suite 4015, Phoenix, AZ 85004, tel. 602/230-7733 or 888/520-3434, fax 602/240-5475, www.arizonaguide.com. CA: Division of Tourism, 801 K St., Suite 1600, Sacramento, CA 95814, tel. 916/322-2881 or 800/862-2543, fax 916/322-3402, www.gocalif.ca.gov. NV: Commission on Tourism, 401 N. Carson St., Carson City, NV 89701, tel. 775/687-4322 or 800/NEVADA-8, fax 800/582-8000, www.travel-nevada.com. NM: Department of Tourism, 491 Old Santa Fe Trail, Santa Fe, NM 87503, tel. 505/827-7400 or 800/545-2070, fax 505/827-7402, www.newmexico.org. UT: Travel Council, Box 147420, Salt Lake City, UT 84114-7420, tel. 801/538-1030 or 800/200-1160, fax 801/538-1399, www.utah.com. For more on the North American deserts and virtually everything in them, visit two excellent Internet resources: www.desertusa.com and www.americansouthwest.net.

CENTRAL CALIFORNIA AND LAS VEGAS
(Great Basin and Mojave Deserts)

Deserts are defined by their extremes: in the weather, in the people who choose to live in them, in the variety of experiences they offer. No desert in the world does extremes better than the Mojave, where you'll find the hottest hot and the most eclectic gathering of eccentric characters in Death Valley, as well as over-the-top gaudiness and edgy excess in Las Vegas, an oasis of glitter surrounded by lonesome-sounding towns like Searchlight, Needles, and Carp. The Mojave gets less than 5 inches of rain a year, and goes from scorching in summer to freezing in winter. The ghost town of Bodie, in the Great Basin Desert, is a much cooler escape year-round. A good way to start off a Death Valley jaunt is to fly into Vegas's McCarran International Airport, explore the casinos awhile, then rent a car and get lost in the desert adventure of your choice. For Bodie, you can fly into San Francisco or Sacramento and rent a car there.

BODIE STATE HISTORIC PARK, NEAR BRIDGEPORT, CA (3A)
Queen of the Ghost Towns, p. 68

Bodie, at an elevation of 8,375 feet, had its brief heyday between 1879 and 1881, following a rich strike of gold and silver. Despite howling winds, subzero winter nights, and snowstorms so severe they cause whiteouts, the population went from 20 to 10,000 virtually overnight, and Bodie began earning its reputation for trouble. A rapid decline set in as mining waned, and over the years fires destroyed most of the town. In 1962, by then completely deserted, it was designated a National Historic Site. Today its 170 buildings are maintained in a state of "arrested decay"; interiors remain as they were when the occupants abandoned them, complete with goods and furnishings. In addition to the museum, one home is open to visitors, and there's a guided tour of a stamp mill. Otherwise, just spring for the $1 self-guided tour and wander this atmospheric ghost town. The park is open year-round, but call for weather-related access information: snow traps many four-wheel-drive vehicles in winter, mud may make the unpaved 3-mi road into town inadvisable in spring, and no towing is available.

CONTACT: Bodie State Historic Park, Hwy. 270, Box 515, Bridgeport, CA 93517, tel. 760/647-6445, fax 760/647-6486, e-mail: bodie@qnet.com, parks.ca.gov/north/sierra/bodie/bshp324.htm; also see ceres.ca.gov/sierradsp/bodie.html. **Bridgeport Chamber of Commerce,** Box 541, Main St., Bridgeport, CA 93517, tel./fax 760/932-7500, www.ca-biz.com/bridgeportchamber.

DISTANCES: 52 mi N of Mammoth Lakes, 20 mi SE of Bridgeport, 45 mi NE of Yosemite National Park

PRICES/HOURS: $1 adults, children free. Open daily 8-7 Memorial Day–Labor Day, 9-4 Labor Day–Memorial Day (weather permitting); museum open daily 10-4 Memorial Day weekend–Labor Day.

OPTIONS: Brush up on your shutter skills at **photography workshops** held at Bodie May through October ($250-$800; contact the park). Steep yourself in Gold Rush history by staying at the 1877 **Bridgeport Inn,** once a popular stage stop on the road into Bodie and now a modest motor hotel with an Irish pub and a restaurant. 205 Main St., Bridgeport, CA 93517, tel. 760/932–7380, fax 760/932–1160, www.thebridgeportinn. com. 31 rooms. Double $50–$60. More intimate, with antiques and down comforters, is the **Cain House B&B**, onetime home of Bodie's biggest landowner and wheeler-dealer. 340 Main St., Bridgeport, CA 93517, tel. 760/932–7040 or 800/433–2246, fax 760/932–7419, www.cainhouse.com. 7 rooms. Double $80–$135 with full breakfast, wine and cheese. No smoking. Closed Nov.–late Apr.

DEATH VALLEY NATIONAL PARK, CA (4–6B–D)
Outer Limits, p. 64

This 3.3 million-acre national park, 50 mi wide by 150 mi long, is the largest outside Alaska. Flanked by mountain ranges on all sides, Death Valley—282 feet below sea level at its lowest point—is famous for being one of the hottest places on the planet. The temperature reached a stunning 134 degrees back in 1913, the second highest ever recorded in the United States. Don't worry, though—normal summer days don't usually get much over 120. Within the park are 14 sq mi of sand dunes, 200 sq mi of salt flats, a volcanic crater 500 feet deep and a half-mile across, and hills, mountains, and canyons of many colors. There's also a museum devoted to the borax once hauled by those 20-mule teams, as well as a unique opera house and a Moorish castle (see "Desert Eccentrics," below). Rangers offer hikes, tours, and talks November through April.

CONTACT: Death Valley National Park, Box 579, Death Valley, CA 92328–0579, tel. 760/786–2331, fax 760/786–3283, www.nps.gov/deva. Visitor center: Hwy. 190.

DISTANCES: Visitor center: 120 mi NW of Las Vegas, 170 mi NE of Barstow, CA

PRICES/HOURS: $10 per car per week. Visitor center open daily 8–6.

OPTIONS: Furnace Creek Inn & Ranch Resort, at the center of the park, has a golf course and its own airstrip. The luxurious Inn, set in a Spanish-style villa, is a popular winter getaway with stars like Martin Sheen and Dennis Hopper. It has a naturally warm spring-fed pool, as does the more casual Ranch, built in the 1800s and filled in summer with European tourists looking to experience the full extremes of Death Valley. Box 1, Death Valley, CA 92328, tel. 760/786–2361 (Inn), 760/786–2345 (Ranch), or 800/236–7916, fax 760/786–2514, www.furnacecreekresort.com. Inn: 64 rooms, 2 suites, some with balcony; tennis courts, bar, restaurant, sauna; double $230–$345, suite $325–$375. Ranch: 224 rooms; 2 restaurants, bar, basketball and tennis courts, stables, gas station; double $97–$174. **Stovepipe Wells Village,** your basic motor inn, is 23 mi northwest of Furnace Creek near the sand dunes and Mosaic Canyon. Hwy. 190, Death Valley, CA 92328, tel. 760/786–2387, www.furnacecreekresort.com/spw.htm. 83 rooms. Restaurant, saloon, pool. Double $40–$80, children under 12 free. **Panamint Springs Resort,** 30 mi west of Stovepipe Wells and so far off the beaten path that it has no phone service, has motel rooms and tent and RV-hookup sites. Box 395, Ridgecrest, CA 93556, tel. 775/482–7680, fax 775/482–7682, www.deathvalley.com/reserve/reserve.html. 14 rooms, 1 cottage. Restaurant/bar. Double $65–$79, cottage $139. There are several other campgrounds in the park; only the tree-shaded one at Furnace Creek takes reservations, which you need if you want a spot during holidays and spring break (tel. 800/365–2267 or online at reservations.nps.gov).

AN OPERA HOUSE AND A CASTLE NEAR DEATH VALLEY, CA (6C, 5C)
Desert Eccentrics, p. 60

Who but an eccentric would choose to live in the heat and solitude, the vast, empty stretches, of the desert? Down in Death Valley, there's no radio, there's no newspaper delivery, and the nearest movie theater is 75 mi away, but like cacti, eccentrics thrive in the desert. Walter Scott set up shop in the valley as a gold prospector, collecting investment money from millionaires for years without ever doing any real prospecting. One, Albert Johnson, spent $2 million building the castle (1922–31; never finished), which Scotty boasted was built with profits from his secret mine. Today rangers in period costume lead 50-minute tours of the place, with its chiming tower, its artworks and European furniture, and its tremendous pipe organ, but leave half a day to see it all. Buy your tickets as soon as you get there—heavy crowds can mean a long wait. Tickets may sell out before noon on holiday weekends. South of here (1½–2 hours) is the Amargosa Opera House, which owes its start to a flat tire: Marta Becket fell in love with the old building she spied while waiting for her flat to be repaired, and the rest is history.

CONTACT: Death Valley National Park, Box 579, Death Valley, CA 92328–0579, tel. 760/786–2331, www.nps.gov/deva; also see www.deathvalley.com. **Death Valley Chamber of Commerce,** 117 Hwy. 127, Box 157, Shoshone, CA 92384, tel. 760/852–4524, fax 760/852–4354, www.deathvalleychamber.org. **Scotty's Castle,** Box 569, Death Valley, CA 92328, tel. 760/786–2392, fax 760/786–2308, www.nps.gov/deva/scotty1.htm. **Amargosa Opera House,** Box 608, Death Valley Junction, CA 92328, tel. 760/852–4441, fax 760/852–4138, www.amargosaoperahouse.org.

DISTANCES: Amargosa is 30 mi SE of Furnace Creek Visitor Center, which is 120 mi NW of Las Vegas, 170 mi NE of Barstow, CA. Scotty's Castle is 54 mi NW of visitor center.

PRICES/HOURS: Amargosa: $12 adults, $8 children 5–12; shows Sat. Oct. and Dec.–Jan., Sat. and Mon. Nov. and Feb.–Apr., 1st 2 Sats. in May, closed June–Sept. (most shows sell out; reservations recommended). **Scotty's Castle:** guided tour $8 adults, $6 seniors, $4 children 6–15; tours daily 9–5, grounds open 7–6.

OPTIONS: You can make Furnace Creek (see Options in "Outer Limits," above) your base camp, or complete the desert-eccentric experience with a stay at the very basic (air-conditioning, but no phones or TVs), year-round **Amargosa Hotel,** attached to the opera house. Built in 1924 to house borax miners, it now has proprietor Marta Becket's murals on the walls of five rooms: try the Jezebel Room, with a swan painted on the headboard and cupids flying around the room, or wake to a trapeze artist flying over your head in the Red Skelton Room. 14 rooms. Double $45–$55.

EUROPEAN ESCAPES IN LAS VEGAS, NV (7D)
City of Illusion, p. 44

To fully experience the incongruities of this most surreal of cities, stay at one of the new European-theme casino hotels—all opulent and marvelous. Bellagio is a major contender for most out of place, with fanny-pack-wearing gamblers discussing buffet options while taking in the traveling exhibitions in the art gallery or the Picassos in the five-star restaurant. Also at the Bellagio are a 116,000-sq-ft casino, a botanical garden, and Cirque du Soleil's "aquatic theater" production, "O"; outside, the fountains put on a show, choreographed to music, several times each hour. The Paris boasts an 85,000-sq-ft casino amid cobblestone streets lined with a patisserie and other French-looking shops, like the gallery where you can watch workers create reproduction art posters. The Venetian's frescoes, Renaissance-costumed staff, canals, and singing gondoliers create a convincing mini-Venice in the desert. (A half-mile gondola ride costs $12.50 for adults, $5 for children; book early in the day—tel. 702/414–4500—as rides sell out.) Its luxurious Canyon Ranch spa has a 40-foot rock-climbing wall, a spa café, and 5 acres of rooftop pools, decks, and gardens. One tip: Vegas sits in the middle of a vast desert, and it can get very warm—try to visit September through April. Tip two: when it comes time to eat, think one word—*buffet.* Grab a plate and line up for all-you-can-eat shrimp, beef sliced while you wait, omelets made to order, dessert bars, you name it, for as little as $10. Other distractions from Vegas's main lure—gambling—include the famous showgirl extravaganzas, amusement-park rides, street entertainments like the Mirage's erupting volcano, shopping at grand casino arcades, quirky museums from wax to Liberace, and sports from the world's largest bowling alley to world-class golf.

CONTACT: Bellagio, 3600 S. Las Vegas Blvd., Las Vegas, NV 89109, tel. 702/693–7111 or 888/987–6667, fax 702/693–8546, www.bellagiolasvegas.com. **Paris,** 3655 S. Las Vegas Blvd., Las Vegas, NV 89109, tel. 702/946–7000 or 888/266–5687, fax 702/946–4405, www.paris-lv.com. **Venetian,** 3355 S. Las Vegas Blvd., Las Vegas, NV 89109, tel. 702/414–1000 or 888/283–6423, fax 702/414–1100, www.venetian.com.

Las Vegas Convention & Visitors Authority, 3150 Paradise Rd., Las Vegas, NV 89109, tel. 702/892–7575, fax 702/892–2824, www.lasvegas24hours.com; also see www.vegas.com, www.lasvegas.com, www.pcap.com. For a map of the Strip, see www.vegas.com/map.html.

DISTANCES: 270 mi NE of Los Angeles, 450 mi SE of Reno, 120 mi SE of Death Valley, 275 mi W of Grand Canyon

FACILITIES: Bellagio: 2,684 rooms, 316 suites, with dataport. 17 restaurants, 6 pools, spa/health club, top-rated golf course (10 minutes away). **Paris:** 2,916 rooms, including 295 suites, with dataport. 8 French-themed restaurants, pool, spa/health club. **Venetian:** 3,036 suites with modem line, fax/printer/copier. 8 restaurants, 5 pools, spa/health club, more than 50 shops.

PRICES: Bellagio: double $159–$759, suite $450–$6,000. **Paris:** double $129–$369, suite $350–$5,000. **Venetian:** suite $109–$599.

OPTIONS: Get married—the idea of doing it in Vegas is just so darned ironic. All the major casinos have ritzy chapels where you can tie the knot. The best way to go, though, is to have Elvis marry you, at the Viva Las Vegas Wedding Chapel (1205 S. Las Vegas Blvd., tel. 800/574–4450, www.vivalasvegasweddings.com) or the Graceland Wedding Chapel (619 S. Las Vegas Blvd., tel. 800/824–5732, www.gracelandchapel.com). If that's too scary, try your hand at **playing poker** in Vegas—just wander back into a casino's poker room, where all the crusty-looking guys are playing seven-card stud and Texas hold-'em. (You can master the game online before you go at www.pokerroom.com.)

CENTRAL CALIFORNIA AND LAS VEGAS HIGHLIGHTS
Head for the Rio resort's rooftop **VooDoo Lounge** for Las Vegas's most excessive drink: What the Witch Doctor Ordered, a 46-ounce concoction spiked with dry ice so it bubbles and steams like a cauldron as you sip it through a fistful of straws. Step onto the 50th-floor balcony to clear your head and get a great view of the Strip. Within an hour of the city is **Hoover Dam** (7D), one of the man-made wonders of the world. You can tour the interior of the structure, which is the height of a 70-story building and two football fields thick at the base, then cool off in Lake Mead. If you're in the Bodie area and you've never mastered floating on your back, try it at **Mono Lake** (3–4 A–B). The 60-sq-mi, mineral-rich lake with "tufa towers" (tall limestone spires) rising up out of it is 2½ times as salty as seawater. Thirty miles south (and open only in summer) is **Devils Postpile National Monument** (3B), one of the coolest geologic formations on the continent. Looking like the pipes of a gigantic church organ, pillars of stone—formed when an ancient 400-foot-deep river of lava dried into polygonal columns—rise 40 to 60 feet off the ground. Just 45 mi southwest of Bodie is **Yosemite National Park** (3A–B), packed with wonders like towering granite peaks, glacial valleys, giant sequoias, and lots of waterfalls, including one of the highest in the world (avoid supercrowded summer).

SOUTHERN CALIFORNIA
(Mojave and Sonoran Deserts)

A good place to experience the desert without roughing it is around Southern California's gold-lamé coast. The resorts of the Palm Springs area define the good life: it's hot, yes (unless baking is your idea of fun, avoid visiting June through September, when the average highs are in the hundreds), but you can always escape into an air-conditioned designer boutique or cool your heels in one of your hotel's handful of pools. You can fly into the Palm Springs Regional Airport, a 1-mi cab ride from the middle of town, or rent a car at Los Angeles International and make the two-hour drive. When you're ready to leave luxury behind, head 90 mi south to Anza-Borrego Desert State Park to experience the area's wilder side. On your way down, you can explore Los Angeles, San Diego, and miles of famed surfing beaches. Visit L.A.'s Farmers Market and Hollywood hot spots, view the human oddities of Venice Beach, take the incredible Pacific Coast Highway drive past the beaches at Huntington Beach, Corona del Mar, and San Clemente. Stop for a quick lunch on a

Laguna Beach clifftop overlooking the Pacific. Draw a breath. And head back out to the desert.

ANZA-BORREGO DESERT STATE PARK, BORREGO SPRINGS, CA (5–6G)
Sounding an Ancient Sea, p. 40

The description of Borrego Paul's "Desert Combo" jeep tour hits the highlights of what this vastly varied, 600,000-acre park has to offer: "Badlands, fossil beds, Indian ruins, canyons, mud caves, earthquake faults, wildflowers, rugged jeep trails, desert plants, and wildlife." In a good spring, parts of the park are a wonderland of wildflowers; the season starts in January and peaks in March. Sometimes the park's bloom reports (tel. 760/767–4684, or see Web site) are accidental poems: "Little Surprise Canyon has windmills, fagonia, and viguiera. You'll find blankets of sand verbena, dune evening primrose, Spanish needles, and the stalks of desert lilies. In the canyons of the Santa Rosas, you may find rock daisy, windmills, and brittlebush in bloom." Cheetahs, sabertooth cats, and camels once ranged through the area's woodland scrub plains. Today 500 mi of dirt roads and 110 mi of riding and hiking trails will introduce you to their replacements: iguanas, golden eagles, kit foxes, muledeer, and bighorn sheep. Sunrises and sunsets at Font's Point draw photographers from around the world; to get there, take Hwy. S-22 12 mi out of town to the Font's Point turnoff, then continue 4 mi south to the parking lot just below the point.

CONTACT: Anza-Borrego Desert State Park, 200 Palm Canyon Dr., Borrego Springs, CA 92004, tel. 760/767–5311, www.anzaborrego.statepark.org. **Borrego Springs Chamber of Commerce,** Box 420, Borrego Springs, CA 92004–0420, tel. 760/767–5555 or 800/559–5524, www.borregosprings.org. **Borrego Paul,** San Diego Outback Tours, Box 1742, Borrego Springs, CA 92004, tel. 760/767–0501 or 888/295–3377, www.desertjeeptours.com.

DISTANCES: 78 mi NE of San Diego, 90 mi S of Palm Springs

PRICES/HOURS: Park: free; visitor center open daily 9–5 Oct.–May, weekends and holidays 9–5 June–Sept. **Tours:** 3 hours $69 per person, 4 hours and sunset evening tours (3 hours with wine or champagne) $89.

OPTIONS: On 42 acres within the park is the plush **La Casa del Zorro Resort,** where carpaccio and portobello are on the menu, golf and tennis are on the to-do list, and jazz rounds out the evening. Most rooms are very large, with patios and fireplaces; two suites have a downstairs living room with grand piano and fireplace. 3845 Yaqui Pass Rd., Borrego Springs, CA 92004, tel. 760/767–5323 or 800/824–1884, fax 760/767–5963, www.lacasadelzorro.com. 44 rooms, 14 suites, 19 1- to 4-bedroom casitas with fireplace, some with private pool or whirlpool. 5 pools, 6 championship tennis courts, 9-hole putting green, fitness spa, stable. Double $135–$375, suite $175–$475, casita $135–$1,225. A stroll away from two canyons and a palm oasis is the **Borrego Valley Inn,** with Southwestern-flavor rooms and spectacular views. 405 Palm Canyon Dr., Box 2524, Borrego Springs, CA 92004, tel. 760/767–0311 or 800/333–5810, fax 760/767–0900, www.borregovalleyinn.com. 14 rooms with private patio, some with fireplace, kitchenette, or whirlpool. 2 pools. Double $110–$165 with breakfast. No smoking. **The Palms at Indian Head** was a favorite haunt of Hollywood stars in the '50s; now it's a funky step back in time—small, plain, and retro, with a bigger-than-Olympic-size pool. 2220 Hoberg Rd., Box 525, Borrego Springs, CA 92004, tel. 760/767–7788 or 800/519–2624, fax 760/767–9717, thepalmsatindianhead.com. 10 rooms. Restaurant, bar. Double $75–$159.

STARRY NIGHTS IN PALM SPRINGS, CA (5F)
Desert Babylon, p. 36

In the mood to just drift? To sip iced drinks through skinny straws, dangle your feet into lukewarm pools? Then it's time for a visit to Palm Springs, where the mission is to indulge, relax, rinse, repeat. Dahling, if you haven't done the Springs, you simply must—this '50s hot spot is chic again, so expect to bump into Hollywood stars and other glamorous types. While you're here, why not take a Celebrity Tour (tel. 760/770–2700; $17) of all the places where Bob Hope, Elvis, and Sinatra liked to hang? Yes, it's cheesy to gawk, but you know you want to.

Walk around the grounds of the Racquet Club (2743 N. Indian Canyon Dr., tel. 760/325–1281), where the villas have plaques dedicated to stars who have checked in over the years: No. 37 is the Spencer Tracy, next to the Joan Crawford and across from the Lucille Ball. If you're feeling ambitious, you could have a game of golf—with 85 courses, this is, after all, one of the world's great golf destinations—or just hang out on Palm Canyon Drive, a palm-tree-lined avenue of galleries, coffeehouses, outdoor cafés, and bars. And don't miss the Follies, which, in addition to the chorus line, features vaudeville-style variety acts (ventriloquists, comics) and headliners like Carol Lawrence, Jo Ann Castle, and the Four Aces.

CONTACT: Palm Springs Visitor and Reservations Center, 2781 N. Palm Canyon Dr., Palm Springs, CA 92262, tel. 760/778–8418 or 800/347–7746, fax 760/325–4335, www.palmsprings.org; also see www.desert-resorts.com, www.palmsprings.com. **Fabulous Palm Springs Follies,** Historic Plaza Theatre, 128 S. Palm Canyon Dr., Palm Springs, CA 92262, tel. 760/327–0225, www.palmspringsfollies.com.

PRICES/HOURS: Follies: $35–$70. Matinees and evening performances Nov.–May; no shows Sun. or Mon. Nov.–Dec., Mon. or Tues. Jan.–May.

DISTANCES: 110 mi E of Los Angeles, 120 mi NE of San Diego

OPTIONS: With its lush grounds and Moorish arches, whitewashed walls and tall palms poolside, the beautifully restored **Korakia Pensione** evokes the glamour of the '20s and '30s, when it was a favorite haunt of the literary crowd. The romantic retreat has been used as a photographic backdrop by everyone from Annie Leibovitz to a gaggle of fashion magazines, and the stars once again gather here. Guest rooms are atmospheric but unfussy, with touches like antiques from Mexico to Afghanistan, old kilims, and black-and-white photos by famous photojournalists. 257 S. Patencio Rd., Palm Springs, CA 92262, tel. 760/864–6411, fax 760/864–4147, www.korakia.com. 2 rooms, 9 studios (with kitchens), 10 suites, 1 cottage, 1 house, no TVs. 2 pools, bocce court, classic movies shown outdoors each night, yoga classes, in-room massages, lunch at pool juice bar, private dinners on request Thurs.–Sun. Double $79–$119,

suite $189–$279, studio and cottage $129–$199, house $395, with full breakfast. **The Willows,** a lavish Mediterranean villa at the foot of the San Jacinto Mountains and in the heart of the village, threatens to drown you in luxury, with its sumptuous antiques, frescoed ceilings, champagne breakfasts, stunning mountain views, and 50-foot waterfall spilling into the pool. 412 W. Tahquitz Canyon Way, Palm Springs, CA 92262, tel. 760/320–0771 or 800/966–9597, fax 760/320–0780, www.thewillowspalmsprings.com. 8 rooms with private patio, dataport. Double $225–$550 with breakfast, evening wine and appetizers. No children under 16, no smoking. Think *The Jetsons,* and you've got an idea of the decor at **The Orbit In,** a '50s hotel full of incredible furnishings by some of the greats who defined Palm Springs style—Eames, Saarinen, Noguchi—in themed rooms like the Rat Pack Suite, Atomic Paradise, and the Leopard Lounge. 562 W. Arenas Rd., Palm Springs, CA 92262, tel. 760/323–3585 or 877/996–7248, fax 760/323–3599, www.orbitin.com. 10 rooms with CD players, VCRs, dataports, private patios, some kitchens. Pool with dataports and bar, whirlpool, complimentary bikes. Double $189–$249 with breakfast, wine in evenings.

THE LIVING DESERT, PALM DESERT, CA (5 F)
The Secrets of Life, p. 34

Re-creating habitats from all four North American deserts, this 1,200-acre park crawls with wildlife: more than 450 animals of 150 species, including coyotes, Mexican wolves, cheetahs, meerkats, and oryx. In Eagle Canyon, watch for golden eagles, mountain lions, and bobcats. The place is set up for families, with eating places, tram tours, and special exhibits like a re-created African village with thatched mud-walled huts, storytellers, and a handicrafts market, as well as camels, hyenas, warthogs, and a "petting kraal" with sheep and goats.

CONTACT: The Living Desert Wildlife & Botanical Park, 47-900 Portola Ave., Palm Desert, CA 92260, tel. 760/346–5694, fax 760/568–9685, www.livingdesert.org.

DISTANCES: 14 mi S of Palm Springs, 120 mi SE of Los Angeles

PRICES/HOURS: $8.50 adults, $7.50 seniors, $4.25 children 3–12 (in summer, $6.50 adults, $3 children). Open daily 8–1:30

mid-June–Aug., 9–5 Sept.–mid-June. Closed Christmas.

OPTIONS: Panoramic views of the desert are fabulous from the **Ritz Carlton,** on a plateau high above the Coachella Valley and just a short drive from The Living Desert. Look for lovely garden displays, a posh spa (natch) with desert-plant treatments, and all the deluxe amenities of a Ritz—you can even request a feather bed. 68-900 Frank Sinatra Dr., Rancho Mirage, CA 92270, tel. 760/321–8282 or 800/241–3333, fax 760/321–6928, www.ritzcarlton.com. 219 rooms, 21 suites, with high-speed Internet access, some private balconies. 3 restaurants, 2 bars, pool, 8 tennis courts, health club, croquet lawn, children's program. Double $169–$425, suite $325–$1,250. Just east of Palm Desert is **La Quinta Resort & Club,** whose lush casita-style accommodations, including suites with private pools and patios, and many amenities will leave you wanting for nothing. 49-499 Eisenhower Dr., La Quinta, CA 92253, tel. 760/564–4111 or 800/598–3828, fax 760/564–5768, www.laquintaresort.com. 920 rooms, 9 suites. 39 pools, 23 tennis courts (hard, grass, clay), tennis clinic, 6 golf courses, 4 restaurants, spa, health club, children's program. Double $99–$585, suite $1,500–$3,000. **Café des Beaux-Arts** (73-640 El Paseo, Palm Desert, tel. 760/346–0669) does a fine imitation of a Parisian sidewalk café with classic French dishes like rabbit Dijonnaise and bouillabaisse.

SOUTHERN CALIFORNIA HIGHLIGHTS

In **Palm Springs** (5F), take the Aerial Tramway up Mount San Jacinto if you're in the mood to hike its 54 mi of beautiful wilderness trails—though, at over 10,000 feet, you could get altitude sickness. Just west of Anza-Borrego and an hour east of San Diego lies **Julian** (5G), a charming former gold-mining town that looks much as it did in frontier days. The tiny town is besieged each October, when its bakers turn out 40,000 delicious pies made with locally grown apples. At other times, it's just a nice, pleasant place to walk about. Be sure to make time to visit **Joshua Tree National Park** (6F), about 40 mi east of Palm Springs. At the meeting of high and low deserts, this ecologically diverse park is named for the extensive stands of strange trees that early settlers thought looked like Joshua raising his arms to heaven.

UTAH AND NORTHERN ARIZONA
(Great Basin Desert)

Stretching between the Rocky Mountains and the Sierra Nevada, the 190,000-sq-mi Great Basin Desert is the largest U.S. desert, covering parts of California, Nevada, Utah, Oregon, and Idaho. With elevations of 3,000 to 10,000 feet, it is colder than the southern deserts; gets about 12 inches of precipitation a year, much of it snow; and has sparser vegetation, like sagebrush and other low scrub. Northern Arizona and southern Utah are full of amazing red-rock landscapes and serene desert views that are among America's most picturesque vistas. Throughout the region—from the Hopi Reservation, with its 12 little villages of stone and adobe perched dramatically atop mesas, to the vast Navajo Nation that surrounds it, to the clifftop dwellings of the Anasazi—you'll find the Native American people, whose history and culture define this land as much as the rocks and mesas do.

HUBBELL TRADING POST, NAVAJO NATION, AZ (12 D)
The Spirit Trail, p. 14

The Hubbell Trading Post, on a 6,340-foot mesa, is the oldest continuously operating one on the 25,000-sq-mi Navajo reservation, and a National Historic Site. It is owned by the National Park Service and operated as a nonprofit along the same lines as when it was established. In addition to watching weaving demonstrations, visitors can shop for baskets, drums, jewelry, and other crafts or take a free guided tour of the Hubbell home, preserved as it was between the 1880s and 1920, with Native American and Western art the famous trader collected. Auctions of Native American arts are held in April and August.

CONTACT: Hubbell Trading Post, Box 150, Ganado, AZ 86505, tel. 520/755–3254 or (park service) 520/755–3475, fax 520/755–3405, navajorugs.spma.org, www.nps.gov/hutr. Post is 1 mi W of Ganado on Hwy. 264. **Navajo Nation Tourism,** Box 663, Window Rock, AZ 86515, tel. 520/871–6436, fax 520/871–7381, www.discovernavajo.bigstep.com; also see www.discovernavajoland.com.

DISTANCES: 39 mi S of Chinle, AZ; 56 mi NW of Gallup, 150 mi NW of Albuquerque, NM

HOURS: Open daily 8–6 May–mid-Sept., 8–5 rest of year. (Note: Arizona is not on Daylight Savings Time, but the reservation is.)

OPTIONS: For a real Navajo experience, stay at one of a handful of **hogan B&Bs.** A hogan, a traditional one-room, eight-sided home of pine logs and earth, has no electricity or running water; bathrooms are usually an outhouse; and guests sleep on simple beds or the dirt floor. Prices start at around $100 a night for two and often include a traditional Navajo breakfast, like blue-corn pancakes. A list of these hogans available from Navajo Nation Tourism (see Contact, above) includes **Two White Rocks Hospitality** (Box 1187, St. Michaels, AZ 86511, tel. 520/871–4360, e-mail: rissawms@hotmail.com; $150 for 2 with breakfast), in the mountains 12 mi northeast of the Hubbell Trading Post, and **Coyote Pass Hospitality** (Box 91-B, Tsaile, AZ 86556, tel. 520/724–3383, www.navajocentral.org/cppage.htm; $100 for 2 with breakfast), 24 mi northeast of the Canyon de Chelly visitor center. Otherwise, the nearest accommodations are in Chinle (see Options in "Listen to the Wind," below) or at the **Navajo Nation Inn,** a basic motel with simple rooms in pine and Southwestern colors. 48 W. Hwy. 264, Window Rock, AZ 86515, tel. 520/871–4108 or 800/662–6189, fax 520/871–5466. 57 rooms. Restaurant. Double $67. More atmospheric is Gallup, New Mexico's **El Rancho Hotel**—a mix of kitsch portraits of movie stars, neon signage, and Old West/Southwest decor. Now owned by a fourth-generation Indian trader, it was built in 1937 by director D. W. Griffith's brother and served as HQ for movies filmed in the area, hosting stars like Katherine Hepburn and Kirk Douglas. 1000 E. Hwy. 66, Gallup, NM 87301, tel. 505/863–9311 or 800/543–6351, fax 505/722–5917, www.elranchohotel.com. 100 rooms with HBO. Restaurant, lounge, pool. Double $43–$76.

CANYON DE CHELLY, CHINLE, AZ (12D)
Listen to the Wind, p. 48

Native Americans have called Canyon de Chelly (pronounced "d'shay") home for more than 2,000 years; about 80 Navajo families farm there today, though most no longer live there. The 130-sq-mi park offers visitors an opportunity to tour the cliff dwellings of the Anasazi, who left the area in the 13th century; examine ancient pictographs that decorate cliff walls; and admire stone formations that rise hundreds of feet above streams, hogans, and tilled fields. Along the 36-mi South Rim Drive are overlooks into the canyon with outstanding views of ruins and features like 800-foot-tall Spider Rock; the 34-mi North Rim Drive has overlooks into the adjacent Canyon del Muerto. To drive on the canyon bottom, a four-wheel-drive vehicle, a free permit, and an authorized Navajo guide are required; it can be hazardous—keep an eye out for deep, dry sand, quicksand, flash floods, and falling rocks. Hiking within the canyon also requires a permit and guide, except along the 2½-mi White House Ruins Trail, which leads to the park's best-known cliff dwelling, with nearly 60 rooms and several kivas. Guides can be hired at Thunderbird Lodge (see Options, below) or the visitor center. Rangers lead hikes and give lectures May through September. Alcohol is prohibited in the park.

CONTACT: Canyon de Chelly National Monument, Box 588, Chinle, AZ 86503, tel. 520/674–5500, fax 520/674–5507, www.nps.gov/cach; also see www.navajoland.com/cdc. Visitor center: 3 mi past Chinle off U.S. 191.

DISTANCES: 36 mi N of Ganado, 50 mi NW of Window Rock, AZ; 97 mi NW of Gallup, NM; 137 mi SE of Monument Valley

PRICES/HOURS: Admission free; hiking with guide, $15 per hour for up to 15 people; driving on canyon bottom with guide, $15 per hour per (your) vehicle. Visitor center open daily 8–5 Oct.–Apr., 8–6 May–Sept.

OPTIONS: The only lodging within the park, besides the free RV and tent campsites, is **Thunderbird Lodge,** a motel partially housed in an 1896 former trading post. Rooms are pleasant, some with rough-hewn beam ceilings, rustic furniture, and

Navajo decor, in buildings of stone and adobe. Half- and full-day jeep tours ($39 and $63.50), as well as horseback and hiking tours, are available. Box 548, Chinle, AZ 86503, tel. 520/674-5841 or 800/679-2473, fax 520/674-5844, tbird lodge.com. 73 rooms. Cafeteria. Double $65-$145, children under 13 free. A few miles away is the **Best Western Canyon de Chelly Inn,** whose clean, spacious rooms so near the canyon sell out from April to October. 100 Main St., Box 295, Chinle, AZ 86503, tel. 520/674-5874 or 800/327-0354, fax 520/674-3715, www.bestwestern.com/canyondechellyinn. 99 rooms. Restaurant, indoor pool. Double $89-$109. For a unique stay at a **hogan B&B,** see Options in "The Spirit Trail," above.

ON HORSEBACK THROUGH MONUMENT VALLEY, AZ/UT (11C)
Riding with the Duke, p. 18

The 17-mi loop of dirt road through the red-rock buttes, mesas, and dunes of the Monument Valley tribal park is one of the most stunning drives on earth, especially at sunset. Rising straight up out of the surrounding flat plain are spires and monoliths of soft shale and sandstone, eroded by wind and rain into fantastic shapes—a bear, three nuns, a totem pole hundreds of feet high. Once home to the Anasazi and now to dozens of Navajo families, the 29,000-acre park is at the junction of northeastern Arizona and southeastern Utah, and part of the Navajo Nation. Outfitters outside the visitor center offer jeep and horseback tours of the valley. Navajo Country Guided Trail Rides has one-hour to several-day rides to remote parts of the valley for a close-up look at Anasazi ruins and rock art.

CONTACT: Monument Valley Navajo Tribal Park, Box 360289, Monument Valley, UT 84536, tel. 435/727-3353, fax 435/727-3353, www.navajonationparks.org/monumentvalley.html. Visitor center: 1 mi E of U.S. 163 at the AZ-UT border. **Navajo Country Guided Trail Rides,** Box 360416, Monument Valley, UT 84536, tel./fax 435/727-3210, www.a-aa.com/trailride.

DISTANCES: Visitor center is 22 mi N of Kayenta (AZ), 175 mi NE of Flagstaff, 300 mi NE of Phoenix.

PRICES/HOURS: Park: $3 adults, children under 8 free; park and visitor center open daily 7-7 May-Sept., 8-5 Oct.-Apr. **Navajo Country trail rides:** 1 hour $25, 3 hours $50, half day $75-$95, overnight $150.

OPTIONS: The pueblo-style buildings of **Goulding's Trading Post and Lodge,** outside the park entrance, blend well with the setting. Balconies overlooking the valley come with all the comfortable, Navajo/Southwestern-look rooms, and the restaurant is decorated with western-movie memorabilia. Off U.S. 163, Box 30001, Monument Valley, UT 84536, tel. 435/727-3231, fax 435/727-3344, www.gouldings.com. 64 rooms, 12 houses. Restaurant, indoor pool, museum. Double $155, house $167. A good, lower-priced alternative 22 mi south of the valley is the bare-bones **Best Western Wetherill Inn.** Box 175, Hwy. 163, Kayenta, AZ 86033, tel. 520/697-3231, fax 520/697-3233. 54 rooms. Double $55-$98.

SLICKROCK MOUNTAIN-BIKE TRAIL, MOAB, UT (12A)
Zoom Zoom Zoom, p. 56

Moab is home to miles of sandstone dunes that grip knobby tires better than your average road and make for great riding. Visit to sample the wide variety of trails, ranging from beginner to daredevil (like Poison Spider and Porcupine Rim); to watch extremely fit fanatics sweat in spandex; to hike gorgeous country; and to see the awesome nearby Arches National Park. The area has been a popular location for films from classic westerns to *Thelma and Louise* (they took that final leap from the Shafer Trail, under Dead Horse Point, near Moab). The 10.3-mi main Slickrock trail has viewpoints overlooking the park, the La Sal Mountains, and the Colorado River—a reminder that Moab is also a center for float and whitewater rafting trips through red-rock canyons.

CONTACT: Moab Chamber of Commerce, 805 N. Main St., Moab, UT 84532, tel. 435/259-7814, www.moabchamber.com; also see discovermoab.com. For maps and info on bike trails: www.moab-utah.com/trails/bikingtrails.html, discovermoab.com/biking.htm. For virtual trail maps, with photos of stops along the way: www.trailmonkey.com/virtual.htm.

DISTANCES: 70 mi N of Blanding, 19 mi W of Castle Valley, 150 mi NE of Monument Valley; 110 mi SW of Grand Junction, CO

OPTIONS: For beginners, **Western Spirit Bike Co.** will organize your trip, lend you a bike, and show you how to ride it. 478 Mill Creek Dr., Moab, UT 84532, tel. 435/259–8732 or 800/845–2453, fax 435/259–2736, westernspirit.com; multiday camping trips $600–$1,000. If all you need is a rental and friendly advice, try one of fanatics' favorite places to slobber over $3,000 bikes: **Poison Spider Bicycles** (497 N. Main St., Moab, tel. 435/259–7882 or 800/635–1792, www.poisonspiderbicycles.com). Meet more enthusiasts at the five-day **Canyonlands Fat Tire Festival** (www.moabfattire.com) in October. Rest weary bones at **Sorrel River Ranch Resort,** on a 240-acre working ranch on the Colorado River—a pricey stay, but the great views of river and buttes might just be worth it. Rooms have vaulted ceilings, red-oak floors, and gigantic log-frame beds. Milepost 17 on Hwy. 128, Box K, Moab, UT 84532, tel. 435/259–4642 or 877/359–2715, www.sorrelriver.com. 33 rooms and suites, all with kitchenette, satellite TV, some with whirlpool, fireplace. Restaurant, pool, fitness center, basketball and volleyball courts, horseback riding, kayaking, rafting, fishing. Rooms and suites $179–$339. No smoking. True to its name, the charming, family-owned **Sunflower Inn** is surrounded by gardens. In downtown Moab, 6 mi from Slickrock and 4 from Arches, the B&B offers antiques-filled rooms, some with balconies and garden patios. 185 N. 300 East, tel. 435/259–2974, fax 435/259–3065, www.sunflowerhill.com. 11 rooms. Outdoor hot tub. Double $85–$175 with breakfast.

UTAH AND NORTHERN ARIZONA HIGHLIGHTS

Like Monument Valley, **Arches National Park** (12A), 5 mi north of Moab, is an amazing, unmissable place. Its balancing rocks, pinnacles, and more than 2,000 natural sandstone arches can be appreciated from a scenic drive or hiking trails. **Bryce Canyon National Park** (9B), about 100 mi NW of Monument Valley, is a small but dazzling park with color-striped spires and rock formations so distinctive that many have been given names, like Sinking Ship, Thor's Hammer, and The Poodle. **Zion National Park** (9B–C), 84 mi SW of Bryce, is home to the world's largest natural arch: 310-foot-long Kolob Arch. If you're interested in Native American jewelry and other arts, slip across the New Mexico border to visit **Gallup** (13D), a walkable town with more than 100 trading posts.

CENTRAL AND SOUTHERN ARIZONA
(Sonoran Desert)

South of the Mojave and north of the Chihuahuan, the Sonoran Desert spans 120,000 sq mi of southwestern Arizona and southeastern California, as well as much of Baja and Sonora, Mexico. The hottest North American desert, it is also the most biologically diverse, thanks to a summer "monsoon" season and winter rains. If you think of deserts as barren, think again. In addition to a wide array of mammals and 58 species of reptiles, the Sonoran is one of the best places in the country to go birding—more than 40 percent of terrestrial bird species spend at least part of the year here. And lording it over a rich mix of desert plants that thrive here is the icon of the desert: the saguaro cactus. Besides Arizona's two biggest cities, Phoenix and Tucson, the region offers natural wonders like the Painted Desert and the Petrified Forest, Indian reservations and petroglyphs, and America's most famous natural attraction: the Grand Canyon.

WHITERIVER, WHITE MOUNTAIN APACHE RESERVATION, AZ (11F)
An Apache Rodeo, p. 30

The 1.6 million-acre White Mountain Apache Reservation is far from everywhere; the drive in from Phoenix, the nearest city, takes about five hours. Still, up to 50,000 people trek each year to the Labor Day Tribal Fair and Rodeo to buy crafts, taste Indian foods, see dance performances by various tribes, and watch Indian cowboys go head to head for prizes of saddles and silver buckles. The five-day celebration also includes basketball and volleyball tournaments, a parade, a carnival, fireworks, and a powwow. The April rodeo,

Canyon Day, is a two-day affair without the trimmings. Fort Apache Historic Park, 5 mi south of Whiteriver, preserves more than 20 buildings of the army post, established in 1870, where Geronimo and a band of Apaches made their last stand. Also on the site are the old military cemetery, prehistoric ruins and petroglyphs, the Cultural Center tribal museum, and a re-created Apache village.

CONTACT: Tribal Fair and Rodeo Office, Box 1709, Whiteriver, AZ 85941, tel. 520/338–4346, ext. 316 or 323. **Apache Office of Tourism,** Apache Cultural Center, Box 507, Fort Apache, AZ 85926, tel. 520/338–1230; see www.wmat.nsn.us/wmacul ture.shtml, www.wmonline.com/attract/discovr.htm. For a map of the reservation, see www.hon-dah.com/rezmap.shtml. **Fort Apache Historic Park,** Box 628, Fort Apache, AZ 85926, tel. 520/338–4625, www.wmat.nsn.us/fortapachepark.htm; for a virtual walking tour, see www.wmonline.com/attract/fta pache.htm. **Pinetop Chamber of Commerce,** Box 4220, Pinetop, AZ 85935, tel. 520/367–4290 or 800/573–4031, fax 520/367–1247, pinetoplakesidechamber.com.

DISTANCES: 30 mi S of Pinetop, 190 mi NE of Phoenix

PRICES/HOURS: Rodeo: $5 per person per rodeo event, various charges for dances. **Fort Apache:** park free; open daily 8–sunset; Culture Center, $3 adults, $2 children 7–14; open Tues.–Sat. 7–4 in summer, weekdays 8–5 rest of year.

OPTIONS: In the little town of Pinetop, at an elevation of 7,200 feet, is **Hon-Dah Resort & Casino,** offering nonstop gambling action (slots, video poker, card room) in a hideaway among the pines. 777 Hwy. 260, Pinetop, AZ 85935, tel. 520/369–0299 or 800/929–8744, fax 520/369–0382, www.hon-dah.com. 128 rooms. Restaurant, lounge with live music, pool with hot tub, sauna. Double $70–$180. **Woodland Inn & Suites** is a quieter alternative, with simple, comfortable rooms and a number of amenities. 458 White Mountain Blvd., Pinetop, AZ 85935, tel. 520/367–3636 or 866/PINETOP, fax 520/367–1543, www.sun ridgehotelgroup.com. 42 rooms with microwave, minifridge, free HBO, some with dataport. Whirlpool room. Double $49–$120 with breakfast.

SEDONA, AZ (10E)
Into the Vortex, p. 22

Whether or not you believe in the healing powers of Sedona's four mysterious vortices, this gorgeous red-rock country has plenty to offer. An abundance of petroglyphs and Native American ruins, like Montezuma's Castle, a 20-room cliff dwelling 30 minutes south; miles of incredible hiking, fishing, mountain biking, hot-air balloon rides, and jeep tours; and lots of massage and spa spots are just the beginning. Add to that 40 galleries of Western and Southwestern art, streets full of trendy and New Age boutiques and bookshops, a collection of sophisticated restaurants, and stunning views of nature at its finest, and you see what lures about 4 million visitors a year to Sedona. Scenic U.S. 89A, which heads north from Sedona through wooded Oak Creek Canyon toward Flagstaff, has been called one of the most beautiful drives in America.

CONTACT: Sedona–Oak Creek Canyon Chamber of Commerce, Box 478, Sedona, AZ 86339, tel. 520/282–7722 or 800/288–7336, fax 520/204–1064, www.sedonachamber.com, www. visitsedona.com; also see www.arizonaguide.com/cities/ sedona/index.html. **Center for the New Age,** 341 Hwy. 179, Sedona, tel. 520/282–2085, www.sedonanewagecenter.com.

DISTANCES: 30 mi S of Flagstaff, 110 mi S of Grand Canyon, 120 mi N of Phoenix

OPTIONS: A luxurious perch practically on top of one of Sedona's power vortices is **The Enchantment Resort.** An award-winning chef presides at the Yavapai Restaurant, where floor-to-ceiling windows give a stunning view of the canyon; the spa offers a dozen kinds of massage and regimens using crystals, ground corn, clay, and cactus. 525 Boynton Canyon Rd., Sedona, AZ 86336, tel. 520/282–2900 or 800/826–4180, fax 520/282–9249, www.enchantmentresort.com. 45 rooms, 88 studios, 60 suites (2 with private pools), 5 haciendas. 2 restaurants, 6 pools, 7 tennis courts, yoga, tai chi, mountain-bike rentals, croquet, bocce ball, table tennis, putting green. Double $350, suite $450–$995, hacienda $655–$1,050. Theme rooms at the cozy **Inn on Oak Creek** offer tasteful decor and huge windows overlooking the creek. 556 Hwy. 179, Sedona, AZ 86336, tel. 520/282–7896 or 800/499–7896, www.sedona-inn.com. 11 rooms with VCR, single or double whirlpool tub, gas fireplace. Double $170–$260 with gourmet breakfast. Try **Heartline Café** (1610 W. Hwy. 89A, tel. 520/282–0785, www.heartlinecafe.com) for great salads like warm red cabbage with hazelnuts and goat cheese, smoked duck with pecans and Gorgonzola, and pistachio-crusted chicken with watercress and sherry vinaigrette—and move on through the fun, eclectic menu from there.

SAGUARO NATIONAL PARK, TUCSON, AZ (10–11H)
The Old Man of the Desert, p. 52

Favored by Snoopy's desert-dwelling brother Spike, the saguaro is the image most likely to come to mind when you think cactus, and Saguaro National Park's got thousands of them. The 91,000-acre park comprises two sites 30 mi apart, one to the east and the other to the west of Tucson. A few precautions are in order: while daytime temperatures average 60 to 70 degrees October through April, highs regularly reach the hundreds May through September. No water is available on most trails, so be sure to come prepared. Watch out for cactus bites, especially from the cholla, which will imbed its spikes in your skin at the slightest touch. And carry a flashlight at night to keep a lookout for rattlesnakes and scorpions. But the park makes it easy to avoid the hazards of the desert—plenty of scenic drives let you tour in the comfort of your air-conditioned car. To catch the sunset from the Gates Pass overlook, take Speedway Boulevard west out of Tucson to Gates Pass Road.

CONTACT: Saguaro National Park, 3693 S. Old Spanish Trail, Tucson, AZ 85730–5699, tel. 520/733–5158 (Saguaro W) or 520/733–5153 (Saguaro E), fax 520/733–5183, www.nps.gov/sagu. For a map of the park and its many hiking trails, see www.gorp.com/gorp/resource/us_national_park/az/map_sa.htm. **Metropolitan Tucson Convention & Visitor's Bureau,** 100 S. Church Ave., Tucson, AZ 85701, tel. 520/624–1817 or 800/638–8350, fax 520/884–7804, www.visittucson.org.

DISTANCES: Saguaro West: 36 mi N of Nogales, 120 mi SE of Phoenix

PRICES/HOURS: Saguaro East, $6 per vehicle; Saguaro West, free. Saguaro East and dirt roads in Saguaro West open sunrise to sunset, paved roads in Saguaro West open 24 hours, both visitor centers open daily 8:30–5.

OPTIONS: Alone amid miles of saguaros is **Casa Tierra,** an adobe hacienda that evokes Old Mexico with its profusion of arches, viga-beam and vaulted brick ceilings, hand-painted tiles, and a plant-filled courtyard that looks out on the desert. Watch the sunset from the hot tub. 11155 W. Calle Pima, Tucson, AZ 85743, tel. 520/578–3058 or 866/254–0006, casatierratucson.com. 3 rooms, 1 2-bedroom suite, with private entrance, patio, minifridge, microwave. Fitness room, telescope. Double $125–$175, suite $175–$300, with gourmet breakfast. 2-night minimum. Closed mid-June–mid-Aug. Two Tom Fazio–designed golf courses sculpted around the contours of the desert (and spiked with saguaros) are the centerpieces of the luxurious, 93-acre **Loews Ventana Canyon Resort.** Other highlights: a renowned restaurant, the Ventana Room, and baths with over-size 2-person tubs. 7000 N. Resort Dr., Tucson, AZ 85750, tel. 520/299–2020 or 800/234–5117, fax 520/299–6832, www.loewshotels.com/ventanahome.html. 371 rooms, 27 suites, with computer jack, minibar, balcony, some with fireplace and whirlpool. 4 restaurants, lounge, 2 pools, 8 tennis courts, 2 golf courses, spa/fitness center, fitness trails, croquet green, children's program. Double $89–$375, suite $229–$2800. Founded in 1868, **Tanque Verde Guest Ranch,** on 640 acres in the foothills of the Rincon Mountains adjoining Saguaro National Park, offers plenty of space for rambling on foot or on horseback—its stable of 140 horses is Arizona's largest. There's a full menu of activities, including outdoor barbecues with a cowboy singer, breakfast horseback rides, and evening events like a Mexican fiesta with mariachi band. 14301 E. Speedway Blvd., Tucson, AZ 85748, tel. 520/296–6275 or 800/234–3833, fax 520/721–9426, www.tanqueverderanch.com. 51 rooms, 23 suites, with modem, minifridge; most with fireplace, private patio. Dining room, lounge, 5 tennis courts, indoor and outdoor pools, saunas, fishing, extensive children's program. Double $260–$450, suite $355–$520, with all meals and activities.

While in Tucson, "Mexican Food Capital of the U.S.," try two top favorites: **La Parrilla Suiza** (5602 E. Speedway Blvd., tel. 520/747–4838; 2770 N. Oracle Rd., tel. 520/624–4300), a small chain specializing in the cuisine of Mexico City, featuring dishes cooked over charcoal or grilled; and **Café Poca Cosa** (88 E. Broadway Blvd., tel. 520/622–6400; closed Sun.), with moles, salsas, and desserts reviewers describe as "exquisite," "bold," and "legendary"—the Plato Poca Cosa is a sampler of the chef's best.

FINDING FRANK LLOYD WRIGHT IN THE ARIZONA DESERT (10G)
An Architect of Nature, p. 24

Of the more than 1,100 works Frank Lloyd Wright designed—from a gas station to the famous house on a waterfall, Fallingwater, to New York's Guggenheim Museum—nearly a third were created during the last decade of his life. Much of that time he spent at Taliesin West. In 1937 he began building the 600-acre complex as a winter home for himself and his wife, Olgivanna, as well as a campus for his architectural-apprenticeship program. In 1987 the U.S. House of Representatives declared Taliesin West a National Historic Landmark, calling it "the highest achievement in American artistic and architectural expression." The school Wright began continues on the site (the grounds are peppered with students' experiments in construction), alongside an architectural firm that carries on Wrightean principles. Besides the Biltmore, which he co-designed with former student Albert Chase McArthur, other Wright sites in the area are Phoenix's First Christian Church (6750 N. 7th Ave.), with its covered walkways and clerestory windows; and the Grady Gammage Memorial Auditorium in nearby Tempe, Arizona State University's performing-arts center, of which Eugene Ormandy, who conducted the inaugural concert in 1964, said, "This is not only the most beautiful room I have ever performed in, but acoustically it is absolutely the finest I have ever experienced." When you go to Phoenix, bring your shades: it gets more than 300 days of sunshine a year, and the average annual temperature is 76 degrees.

CONTACT: Frank Lloyd Wright Foundation, Taliesin West, 12621 Frank Lloyd Wright Blvd., Box 4430, Scottsdale, AZ 85261–4430, tel. 480/860-2700, fax 480/451–8989, www.franklloydwright.org. **Greater Phoenix Convention & Visitors Bureau,** 400 E. Van Buren, Suite 600, Phoenix, AZ 85004, tel. 602/254–6500 or 877/225–5749, fax 602/253–4415, www.phoenixcvb.com.

PRICES/HOURS: 1-hour tours winter/summer, $16/$12 adults, $12.50/$10 seniors and students, $4/$3 children 4–12 (also available: 1½-, 2-, and 3-hour tours and evening tours on Fridays). Tours daily at 9, 10, 11 AM May–Oct. (closed Tues.–Wed. July–Aug.), every ½ hour 10–4 Nov.–Apr.

DISTANCES: 15 mi E of Phoenix, 120 mi NW of Tucson

OPTIONS: The **Arizona Biltmore Resort & Spa** has been dramatically expanded since its 1929 opening, but Wright's aesthetic is reflected in the Mission-style furnishings and soothing palette of beige and sand colors. Accommodations exude an air of relaxed, refined comfort, including very spacious "villa suites" with full kitchens and living rooms with gas fireplaces. Recent additions are a spa complex offering more than 80 treatments, and a pool with a 92-foot water slide and waterfall. 2400 E. Missouri Ave., Phoenix, AZ 85016, tel. 602/955–6600 or 800/950–0086, fax 602/381–7600, www.arizonabiltmore.com. 736 rooms, 18 suites, 65 villa suites, most with balcony. 4 restaurants, 8 pools (1 Olympic-size), fitness center, 24-hour business center, children's program, putting course; 2 adjacent golf courses. Double $145–$550, suite $295–$1,000, villa suite $575–$1,250. Turkish rugs, French windows, Italian frescoes, and other lavish touches greet you at every turn at **Royal Palms Hotel and Casitas,** centered on a Spanish Colonial–style mansion built in 1929. 5200 E. Camelback Rd., Phoenix, AZ 85018, tel. 602/840–3610 or 800/672–6011, fax 602/840–6927, www.royalpalmshotel.com. 34 rooms, 35 suites, 4 villa suites, 43 casitas, most with balcony and fireplace. Restaurant, poolside grill, bar, pool, tennis court, fitness center, in-room massages, bike rentals, croquet. Double $159–$495, suite $179–$3,500, casita $199–$495.

CENTRAL AND SOUTHERN ARIZONA HIGHLIGHTS
Sedona is just 34 mi from the charming college town of **Flagstaff** (10E). A walk through its Rockwellian streets is well

worth a day trip. **Tucson** (10H) is another charming and eminently walkable college town; start a tour at the Tucson Museum of Art and Historic Block, which features a handful of the town's original buildings and a cathedral built in the 1890s. At vast **Lake Powell** (10–11 B–C), 85 mi north of Flagstaff amid a million acres of desert, you can glide through stunning red-rock canyons between towering rock formations on a houseboat, stopping to sun on secluded beaches and swim the clear waters. Sedona is also just 115 mi south of the **Grand Canyon** (8–10 C–D), one of North America's absolute must-sees: 277 mi long, 18 mi across at its widest spot, and more than a mile deep, with panoramic views that truly take your breath away. Though the North Rim is harder to get to than the South Rim—the trip is longer, and snow can close roads—it's at a higher elevation and so it's cooler, it's covered in pine woods, it offers views into the harshly beautiful Painted Desert, and it gets you away from the crowds and back-to-back RVs. Deer here are largely unafraid of humans, and you'll catch them grazing in meadows at the side of the road. A whitewater rafting trip down the Colorado River through the canyon is an unforgettable adventure.

SOUTHERN NEW MEXICO
(Chihuahuan Desert)

Much of the 200,000-sq-mi Chihuahuan Desert is south of the border; the rest covers parts of New Mexico, Texas, and southeastern Arizona. Cool in winter and scorching in summer, this desert does not boast a broad variety of plant life but does have one claim to fame: it has more types of cactus than any other region, along with its characteristic shrubs, yuccas, and agaves. Southern New Mexico is where you'll find the enchanting Carlsbad Caverns, numerous Anasazi cliff dwellings, the Petroglyph National Monument, and the ethereal White Sands, as well as the quintessentially Southwestern town of Santa Fe, the artsy enclave of Taos, and the outdoor-activities mecca of Silver City, an old silver-mining boomtown at the edge of the Gila Wilderness.

HATCH CHILE FESTIVAL, HATCH, NM (14H)
A Pandemonium of Peppers, p. 72

Hatch has good reason to call itself the Chile Capital of the World: the tiny village is at the heart of a region that grows much of New Mexico's annual $60 million chile crop. The festival features a parade, a cook-off, the crowning of the Chile Festival Queen, a fiddling contest, and a barn dance, with carnival and pony rides for kids. This is your chance to load up on a year's worth of excellent chiles, grown in what many diehard fans consider the Napa Valley of chile. If you're *really* into chiles, check out the Teaching and Demonstration Garden at the Chile Pepper Institute, headed by one of the world's leading chile breeders, at the state university at Las Cruces; April through October, you can clap your eyes on 150+ varieties of exotic chiles, some invented right here (look for the purple ones).

CONTACT: Hatch Valley Chamber of Commerce, Box 38, Hatch, NM 87937, tel. 505/267–5050. For more information on the Chile Festival, tel. 505/267–1343; also see www.zianet.com/snm/hatch.htm. **Chile Pepper Institute,** NMSU Box 30003, NMSC 3Q, Las Cruces, NM 88003, tel. 505/646–3028, www.chilepepperinstitute.org; garden off University Ave.

DISTANCES: 36 mi NW of Las Cruces, 189 mi SW of Albuquerque

OPTIONS: In Mesilla, a charming village of cobbled streets with a Mexican-style plaza 2 mi south of Las Cruces, is the **Meson de Mesilla,** a warm B&B with a three-star Continental restaurant and great views of mountains and mesas. 1803 Avenida de Mesilla, Box 1212, Mesilla, NM 88046, tel. 505/525–9212 or 800/732–6025, fax 505/527–4196, www.mesondemesilla.com. 14 rooms, 1 suite, with dataport, some with minifridge or fireplace. Restaurant, cocktail lounge, pool. Double $65–$92, suite $135–$140, with full breakfast. No smoking. The **Hilltop Hacienda B&B** is a secluded adobe-brick home with spacious rooms, 18 acres to explore, and a perfect hilltop location that offers serene views of Las Cruces, the valley, and the mountains. 2600 Westmoreland, Las Cruces, NM 88012, tel. 505/382–3556, www.zianet.com/hilltop. 3 rooms. Double $65–$75 with full breakfast. No smoking. Allegedly haunted and rumored to have once been a bordello, the Prairie-style **T.R.H. Smith Mansion Bed & Breakfast** was built in 1914 for a local banker and embezzler. Highlight: a pool room with a 9-foot vintage pool table. 909 N. Alameda Blvd., Las Cruces, NM 88005, tel. 505/525-2525 or 800/526-1914, fax 505/524-8227, www.smithmansion.com. 4 rooms. Double $60–$132 with full German breakfast. No smoking. A stop is mandatory at **B&E Burritos** (300 Franklin, Hatch, tel. 505/267-5191) for heavenly burritos and chile stew, and at **Nellie's Café** (1226 W. Hadley Ave., Las Cruces, tel. 505/524-9982) for brilliant versions of basics like flautas and chiles rellenos. Mesilla's **La Posta** (2410 Calle de San Albino, tel. 505/524-3524, www.laposta-de-mesilla.com) serves up "New Mexico Mexican" dishes and char-broiled steaks in a historic setting: a stagecoach stop from the 1840s.

WHITE SANDS NATIONAL MONUMENT, ALAMOGORDO, NM (15 G–H)
A Storm on the Sand Sea, p. 8

There's a nice 16-mi round-trip drive through White Sands, as well as short nature trails and a long boardwalk, but the more adventurous will want to hike down the Alkali Flat Trail (4.6 mi round-trip) into the heart of the sands. Wade barefoot through what is the largest deposit of gypsum sand in the world (the crystals don't get hot), climb to the top of the dunes, then tumble down them—or surf down on a plastic saucer sold at the visitor center. If you do hike, remember what folks there keep telling you: there is no water in the park. You'll be out under a hot sun, one dune pretty much looks the same as the next, and the wind can quickly wipe out your tracks. And there is no water, see? The message being: bring plenty of water. Also a compass. Strong winds may make it impossible to visit the dunes, and testing at the nearby missile range sometimes forces road closures, so call ahead to make sure the park's open.

CONTACT: White Sands National Monument, Box 1086, Holloman AFB, NM 88330 (visitor center: 19955 Hwy. 70W), tel. 505/679-2599 or 505/479-6124, fax 505/479-4333, www.nps.gov/whsa; also see www.zianet.com/snm/whit sand.htm, www.zianet.com/snm/whsand1.htm. **Alamogordo**

Chamber of Commerce, 1301 N. White Sands Blvd., Alamogordo, NM 88310, tel. 505/437-6120 or 800/826-0294, fax 505/437-6334, www.alamogordo.com.

DISTANCES: 15 mi SW of Alamogordo, 52 mi NE of Las Cruces

PRICES/HOURS: $3 per person per week. Visitor center open daily 8–7 Memorial Day–Labor Day, 8–4:30 rest of year. Dunes Drive open daily 7–9 in summer, 7–sunset rest of year.

OPTIONS: A comfortable, just-the-basics stop at the crossroads of Highways 54, 70, and 82 is the **Best Western Desert Aire Motor Inn.** 1021 S. White Sands Blvd., Alamogordo, NM 88310, tel. 505/437-2110, fax 505/437-1898. 90 rooms, 9 suites, with minifridge, modem line. Pool, sauna, game room. Double $52–$109, suite $65–$119, with Continental breakfast. Escape the heat of Alamogordo, 15 minutes away, amid the pines at the **Good Life Inn Bed and Breakfast,** a cozy inn beside a stream in the mountains. 164 Karr Canyon Rd., Box 711, High Rolls, NM 88325, tel. 505/682-5433 or 866/543-3466, www.goodlifeinn.com. 3 rooms with minifridge, microwave, coffeemaker, 200-channel TV/VCR, CD player. Living room with wide-screen TV and fireplace, billiard/game room, small Jacuzzi/fitness room. Double $102–$155 with full breakfast and happy hour.

SOUTHERN NEW MEXICO HIGHLIGHTS
The **International Space Hall of Fame** in Alamogordo (15G) has a planetarium, an IMAX theater, plus satellites, spacesuits, rockets, missiles, moon rocks, and other space stuff. The amazing **Carlsbad Caverns National Park** (16–17H), 135 mi southeast of White Sands, has more than 80 limestone caves full of fascinating formations, from massive stalagmites and stalactites to fragile cave pearls, draperies, popcorn, and lily pads. Late May to mid-October, watch as tens of thousands of bats exit the caverns at sunset. Near Deming, an hour west of Las Cruces, lies the rock hunter's dream: **Rock Hound State Park** (14H). Unlike most U.S. parks, this one allows visitors to take home natural souvenirs; unfortunately, the area is so picked over it can take a lot of time, chiseling, and perseverance to find good ones, like jasper, geodes, and shiny black perlite. Bring your shovel.

Author David Lansing dangles his feet in the saline waters off Newport Beach, California, where he lives with his wife and two children, but pines for the vast open spaces and tranquillity of Southwestern deserts, where he frequently flees when he wants to be alone. Which is often. His story "Confessions of a Cheese Smuggler," first published by *National Geographic Traveler*, where he is a contributing editor, was included in *The Best American Travel Writing 2000*. His work has also won journalism awards for *Sunset, Orange Coast,* and *The Los Angeles Times*. When he grows up, he'd like to be a filmmaker and live in Paris.

Born and raised in Hong Kong, San Francisco–based Catherine Karnow is one of the world's most sought-after editorial photographers. After a brief career as a filmmaker, she turned to still photography, and has been working professionally full time for 16 years. Her work appears frequently in *National Geographic Traveler, Smithsonian,* French and German *GEO,* and countless other publications, including several *Day in the Life* book projects. Karnow was among 70 leading international photojournalists chosen to work on the book *A Passage to Vietnam*. She also contributed to the book *Women in the Material World*.